EUREKA!

S. Ananthanarayanan was a student of physics who strayed into the world of newspapers, banking and then the civil services. But he stayed committed to the sciences and the dissemination of science, and has brought current developments in the sciences to lay newspaper readers through a weekly column since the year 2001.

In an earlier book, *Icons from the World of Science*, he describes to the general reader the work of ten Indian scientists. In recognition of his work, in the year 2007, he received a national award for science communication from the Department of Science and Technology, Government of India.

EUREKA!

Greatest Scientists
Who Changed the World

S. ANANTHANARAYANAN

RUPA

Published by
Rupa Publications India Pvt. Ltd 2019
7/16, Ansari Road, Daryaganj
New Delhi 110002

Sales Centres:
Allahabad Bengaluru Chennai
Hyderabad Jaipur Kathmandu
Kolkata Mumbai

ISBN: 978-93-5333-545-8

First impression 2019

10 9 8 7 6 5 4 3 2 1

The moral right of the author has been asserted.

Printed at HT Media Ltd, Gr. Noida

To Hemant Kumar Banerji,
Iconic science teacher at
St Aloysius High School, Jabalpur

Contents

Preface

It is the sum total of ideas and knowledge, rather than monuments or empires, which constitutes the durable asset created by humanity. While literary and artistic talent has flourished in all parts of the world, the scientific legacy, which defines the modern world, has followed a path that begins with the ancient Greeks.

The pages that follow are short accounts of the works of leading lights along the way. The scientists are arranged from the earliest to the most recent, to show how ideas progressed over the ages. The list is by no means complete, but the sixty scientists who have been described represent the main torchbearers in the fields of mathematics, astronomy, mechanics, electricity, magnetism, the nature of materials and the atom, physiology, genetics and medicine.

In the decades to come, the world has to combat a serious challenge—global warming and environmental pollution. Behavioural and lifestyle changes would be necessary, but what may finally help the human race to cope is its scientific strength.

This book is an effort to bring to the general reader some of the principal concepts in the sciences, and glimpses of how they came to be.

Pythagoras

The modern world has to thank the ancient Greeks for many things. From the genre of tragedy in literature, the Olympics in sports and democracy as a form of government, the Greek influence has shaped growth in the Western World. But the most enduring and consequential influence was surely the Greek contribution to formal mathematics and the scientific method.

The Greeks sought to find structures and regularity in what was beautiful and natural. They thought deeply about lines, angles, shapes, areas and volumes. They found order in the movement of the stars and the planets, and tried to discover a mathematical basis that ruled them. But above all, Greek society allowed unusual and independent thinkers to thrive. These persons, who bent their minds to understand the world around them, have left for us both a treasure trove of ideas as well as a discipline of how to discover the ways of nature. Their influence guided the course of seekers of truth for many centuries.

Pythagoras was a legendary philosopher and thinker of Greece in sixth century BCE. He was born in the city of Samos in Ionia, and even as a young man, became learned in geometry, arithmetic, astronomy and religion. His ideas and associations, however, appear to have created social tensions that may have forced him to leave Samos for the Greek colony of Croton (in modern day Italy). Even at Croton, his school of thinkers, called the Pythagoreans, invited opposition, and though Pythagoras lived to a ripe old age, he may have ultimately perished in an uprising against him and his group.

Pythagoras is immortal as the one who formally laid down the powerful mathematical deduction—the Pythagoras Theorem—although the Babylonians and Indians had some related ideas. The theorem is a relationship among the three sides of a triangle whose one angle is a right angle. As Figure 1 shows, any triangle can be easily divided into a pair of right-angled triangles. For this reason, Pythagoras' theorem has wide application and can be used to establish a relationship among the sides of any shape that is made up of straight lines.

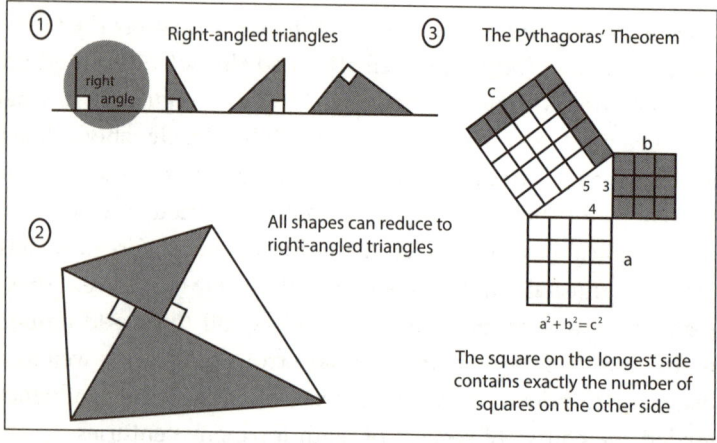

Figure 1

A right angle is also a quarter of a circle. Figure 2 shows that all kinds of right-angled triangles get created when the radius moves around the circle. As the Pythagoras Theorem creates a relationship between the sides of the triangles that are formed by the moving radius of the circle, it helps us in measuring a circle and the angles that the radius makes when it moves. This has made the Pythagoras Theorem an important formula in engineering, wave motion, optics and electronics.

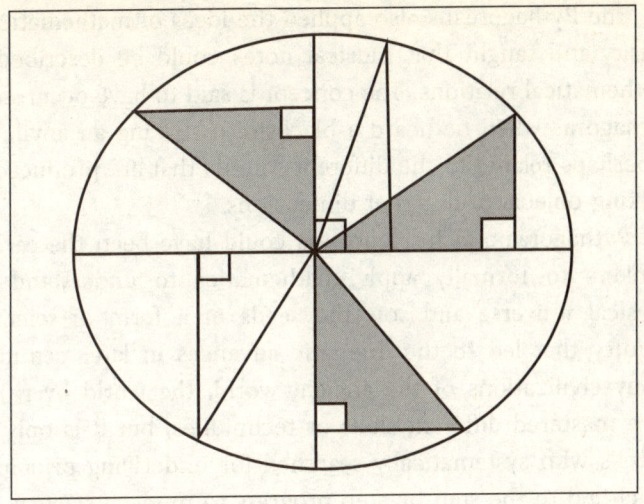

Figure 2

The Pythagoreans themselves were a group of Greek philosophers who made the pursuit of truth and order a way of life, and often lived apart from others who followed humdrum vocations. They espoused ideas of personal freedom, justice and simplicity in living and many of them were vegetarians. Though they had built the ideological foundation of the city states, their exclusivity ran counter to democratic ideas and they were often at loggerheads with political forces. They are credited with scientific insight, including an early belief that the earth was spherical; that it was divided into five climatic zones; and that the morning and the evening star were the same—the planet Venus. As geometers, they believed that the heavenly bodies moved in circles, strongly influencing future thinkers in this area. Even Copernicus—who showed that it was not the earth, but the sun, which was the centre of 'the heavens'—admitted that he had been influenced by Pythagorean ideas.

The Pythagoreans also applied the ideas of mathematics to music, and taught that musical notes could be described by mathematical relations. The concept is said to have occurred to Pythagoras when he heard a blacksmith striking an anvil, and is perhaps related to the different sounds that are produced by striking objects of different dimensions.

Pythagoras and his followers could have been the earliest thinkers to formally apply mathematics to understand the physical universe and sow the seeds of a form of scientific enquiry that led to the dramatic advances in later centuries. Many civilizations of the ancient world, the world over, may have mastered different skills or techniques, but it is only the Greeks who systematically searched for underlying principles, which led to the step-by-step progress to modern science.

Euclid

Can we learn to think the same way that we learn to write or drive? It does seem that we can, as there is a method to thinking and reasoning. Mental processes, which led to progress in science and technology, modern economy, law, and even aspects of art and literature, seem to have been guided by a process of logic that was developed in ancient Greece.

There was a celebrated Greek who saw a pattern, progression and system in the way his contemporaries thought about lines, shapes and volumes, and he collected their work in a book, whose content remains almost unchanged to this day.

This man was Euclid, who lived around 300 BCE, when his book appeared. We know very little about him, but we do know that he taught mathematics in Alexandria, Egypt. His book—a treatise on geometry, called *Elements*—was translated from the original Greek into Arabic and then into Latin, and this is the version that has survived.

Although Alexandria is in Egypt, it was the Greek, Alexander the Great, who founded Alexandria in 331 BCE. Alexandria soon grew into an important commercial and academic centre. With its great library, it was the intellectual and cultural capital of the ancient world and attracted scholars from far and near. Alexandria was also the Greek gateway to the delta of the Nile. The Nile, which overflowed its banks every year, covered the country with fertile soil and the land was rich and prosperous. But the annual flooding also changed boundaries of landholdings and it was necessary to redistribute the land among the owners. The Egyptians had hence developed basic geometry for measurement of area, which they used to manage the land, to calculate taxes and for trade. In fact, the word 'geometry' arises from the Greek words 'gē' (which means the earth) and 'metria' (which means the science of measuring).

However, the Greeks, who had had links with Egypt since a long time, looked deeper into the latter's techniques of demarcating areas of land. Thales, a Greek thinker of the seventh century BCE, was the first to conceive of geometry as a science. Thales systematically used geometrical methods, like the ratio of an object's height and its shadow, to calculate the height of pyramids and the distance of a ship from the shore. Thales is the first on record to look for reasons other than mythology to explain everyday things and it is said that he kept records of the weather and could predict a good harvest!

Others soon followed Thales in the contemplation of ideas of geometry. A number of thinkers and philosophers, until the third century BCE, strove to find rational explanations for the ways of nature. Notable among these are Hippocrates and Pythagoras. The philosophical leaders of the age included Plato, who founded the Academy at Athens, and Aristotle, who was tutor of Alexander the Great and influenced thinkers for centuries.

Along with enquiry into nature, and subjects that included the properties of numbers, shapes and quantities, the mysteries of the night sky, and even law and ethics, there grew a tradition of systematic thinking. This method, which was first used in mathematics, began with considering what we know or believe to be true, and following a chain of reasoning, to arrive at other truths that are not so obvious. By the third century BCE, when Euclid was active, there was a considerable body of work that had been done by different mathematicians in Greece and elsewhere (in the Arab world, for instance). Euclid undertook the task of collecting the different results about lines and shapes—the subject matter of geometry—and put them together in a logical sequence. He refined the available material by providing definitions of concepts such as a straight line, a point or a triangle, and pinpointing relationships that could be just taken to be true. A straight line was defined as 'that which lies evenly between two points', and an example of something taken to be obvious (an axiom) is that 'the whole is greater than any of its parts' or 'any two points can be connected by a straight line'.

In this way, Euclid brought together the different properties of lines, angles, triangles, squares, circles, and the like, which had been deduced by thinkers over the years and at different places, often with no communication among them. He arranged the discoveries in order, with the simplest results or theorems first, and then the results that had been arrived at based on the earlier results. He refined the statement and proof of the results by explicitly stating the propositions and the assumptions, and clearly expressing each line of proof as a result of the previous one. And where some results had not been proved, Euclid himself worked out the proof to make the sequence consistent. The final product was then a progression of the fundamental and proven properties of lines and shapes, which has been the basis for all science, engineering, astronomy, surveying, architecture, town planning and navigation, ever since. The content of the geometry textbooks used today in schools in every country is practically the same as Euclid wrote down twenty-three centuries ago.

What is important in Euclid's *Elements* is that along with useful geometric results, each proof of mathematical ideas expresses the essential features found in logical deduction. From a given set of facts or assumptions, the proof follows successive consequences of the facts, either self-evident or the result of an earlier proven fact, to arrive at a final, non-obvious, but useful fact. The procedure starts with stating a proposition or a relationship that is not obviously correct in all cases. The procedure then recalls what is known to be true, and then, by reasoned steps, moves to the proposition itself, or a conclusion that cannot be true unless the proposition is also true.

The method has application not only in mathematics, but also in deciding questions of rights or obligations, of solving a crime or of devising acceptable rules or laws. When the Euclidian method is used in matters relating to society and human relations, the actors in the issue are depersonalized, or replaced by symbols that have only the qualities essential to the matter. For instance, in deciding the rights of one's kinsman in a property dispute, one will consider what rights should be enjoyed by any individual, not necessarily one's kinsman. Our judgement is then not clouded by our relationship and it is easier to decide the matter.

It was this aspect of objectivity that Euclid's study provided, and hence, over the centuries, persons trained in geometry were called upon to solve issues of law or equity. After these fertile years and a century or so after the time of Euclid, the spirit of enquiry in the European world lay dormant for over a millennium. But finally, when it flowered again during a period of reawakening known as the Renaissance in fourteenth century CE, it was the seed planted by the Greeks that had germinated.

Archimedes

'Give me the place to stand, and I shall move the earth,' is a line credited to Archimedes, of the third century BCE, in Greece, in describing the principle of the lever.

Archimedes, a scientist, mathematician and inventor, is the epitome of the vibrant intellectual life in ancient Greece. Archimedes, the son of Phidias, a Greek astronomer, was born around 287 BCE in Syracuse, in Sicily. He studied mathematics in the renowned school at Alexandria, as the contemporary of Conon of Samos, a student of Euclid and a leading mathematician and astronomer of the time.

While Archimedes trained in the tradition of seeking truth by pure reasoning, he became associated with the royal family of Syracuse and matters of the state, and turned his mind to practical applications too. Legend has it that King Hiero II of Syracuse wished to confirm that a quantity of gold given to a goldsmith to fashion a crown had all been used for the crown. The question was really one of finding out the volume of the crown, but this was not possible by measurement, as the crown had no regular shape. Archimedes is said to have found the solution when he lowered himself into a bath and noticed that the level of water rose. He realized that the amount of water that an object displaced when it was submerged has exactly the volume of the object. All that had to be done to know the volume of the crown was to immerse the crown in water and see how far the water rose. It is said that the crown was found to weigh less than it should have. As silver weighs only half as much as an equal volume of gold, the goldsmith was found to have mixed silver with the gold.

An important discovery that Archimedes had made while solving the case of the dishonest goldsmith was that when the crown was immersed in water, it weighed less than it had before. The reduction in the weight, in fact, was the same as the weight of the water displaced. As we know that water weighs 1 g for every cm^3, we can now find out the volume of an object simply by weighing it in air and then in water, without measuring the volume of water displaced.

This is the idea that is now known as Archimedes' principle— truly a breakthrough in understanding what every shipbuilder or anyone who had learnt how to swim knew intuitively. But with the principle in place, ships, barges and other floating craft could be designed as required, in place of being built by a method of trial and error. The principle also explained how things that live underwater were able to move up or down. The volume of an iceberg could be worked out from the part visible above the water and how much load a ship could safely take could be estimated in advance.

While working in the court of Hiero, Archimedes bent his mind to all kinds of practical things, both for everyday use as well as for use in war. He is said to have invented the Archimedes' screw, a device for raising water, which is still used as a pump to drain marshes. He also developed machines to lift loads, and applications of the humble lever and the pulley block, which are used in cranes and earthmoving equipment to this day.

More to the interest of the State of Syracuse were the military instruments. These ranged from improved catapults and artillery to mechanical monsters like the Claw of Archimedes, a suspended hook that could grasp and capsize invading ships.

Once, when Syracuse was under siege by the Roman navy, Archimedes set up large metallic mirrors that focused sunlight onto enemy ships and set the sails on fire. Roman soldiers must have been terrified at the defenders' high-tech tactics that were centuries ahead of their time!

For all these achievements of engineering and technology, Archimedes was a theoretician in the Greek tradition and he made important contributions to basic science and mathematics. He discovered the principle of the lever, that a small force at a large distance from the fulcrum could move a large load placed closer to the fulcrum. A more complex configuration was with a system of pulleys, where a small effort moving through a larger distance could lift a large load. This is the principle of the machines and systems or gears that multiply effort and drive the powerful engines of the modern world.

The greatest work of Archimedes, however, is still in the field of mathematics. He made the most accurate estimate of his time—of the value of Pi: the ratio of the circumference of a circle to its diameter—using a method that is purely numerical and not geometrical. The estimates of Pi had all been by actual measurement of the circumference and diameter of circles, or by comparing a circle and a many-sided figure that was almost the circle. These methods, however, were finally only approximations. Archimedes's method involved no measurement and, in principle could get continuously more accurate.

Archimedes started by drawing a regular hexagon (a six-sided figure) around a circle, so that the sides of the hexagon touched the circle (see Figure 3). Euclid had written down a formula that could be used to calculate the ratio of the perimeter of the hexagon to the diameter of the circle. Archimedes ingeniously extended the formula to consider the perimeter of a figure with 12, 24, 48 and 96 sides. Next, he did the same with a hexagon, going to a multisided figure, but inside the circle, rather than on the outside. The perimeters of the two multisided figures, outside and inside the circle, are then the upper and lower limits of the circumference of the circle itself.

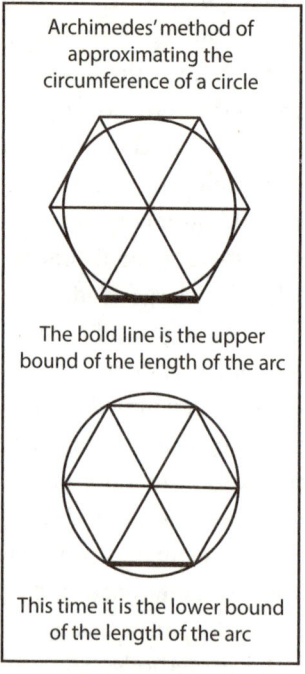

Archimedes' method of approximating the circumference of a circle

The bold line is the upper bound of the length of the arc

This time it is the lower bound of the length of the arc

Figure 3

In principle, the process of subdividing the multisided figure can extend to figures with 192 sides, 384 sides, and so on, to give us closer and closer lower and upper limits of the length of the circumference, and thereby of the value of Pi.

Archimedes used similar methods of great sophistication to estimate other mathematical results that had no exact solutions, for instance, the value of the square root of 3. He did computations of the ratio of the areas and volumes of geometric figures in two and three dimensions (see Figure 4) and also proved the well-known formula for the area of a circle.

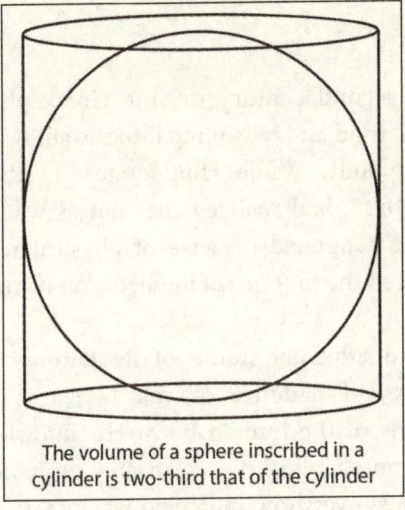

The volume of a sphere inscribed in a cylinder is two-third that of the cylinder

Figure 4

A famous work of Archimedes is his investigation into how many grains of sand the universe could hold. While this predates some current attempts at computing the number of atoms in the universe by over two millennia, the work is also a first in the system of naming very large numbers. The system devised is, in fact, the method of using exponents, like 10 to the power of 10, which is written as 10^{10}. Archimedes raised the number 10^8 to the power of 10^8 and then again to the power of 10^8 and so on. That Archimedes could do this is remarkable, as the Greek system of numerals was not what we have today; it employed twenty-seven different letters of the Greek alphabet, nine letters for the units from 1 to 9, nine letters for the tens from 10 to 90 and nine letters for the hundreds from 100 to 900.

Galen

During the second century CE, the Greek physician Galen brought method and reasoning into the study and treatment of the human body. While Hippocrates, in the fourth and fifth centuries BCE, had realized that illness was not heavenly retribution but happened because of physical reasons, it was Galen who placed the practice of medicine on firm, experimental bases.

He carried out detailed studies of the anatomy of animals and body processes and made use of what he learnt to understand the mechanisms of the human body. His knowledge and skill made him an outstanding physician and surgeon of his times and his influence over how medicine was practised dominated for over a millennium

Galen was born in 130 CE in Pergamon, a city in ancient Mysia, in western Asia Minor, then part of the Roman Empire. The city had a library that was second only to Alexandria's, and Galen's father, Aelius Nicon, was a wealthy farmer, educated in philosophy, mathematics and the physical sciences. Galen's upbringing was hence rich and inspiring. It is said that in the course of a serious illness, which Galen recovered from, his father had a dream that the boy be made a physician. At the age of seventeen, accordingly, Galen began to train in medicine. Galen soon moved to Alexandria, where the legendary Hippocrates had taught, and over several years, he absorbed medical knowledge from the best known teachers in the field.

The practice of medicine of the time was generally passive management to allow the body to overcome the disease in the natural course of time. The Hippocratic tradition, no doubt, had separated medicine from religion and had introduced a degree of analysis. But physicians of the time still believed that it was four kinds of body fluids—blood, yellow bile, black bile and phlegm—called the four humours, whose balance affected mood, emotion and behaviour. The young Galen, however, had been exposed to the philosopher Aristotle and he valued the methods of observation and experiment. Galen had closely followed Aristotle's writings on biology and had a grasp, from early years spent on his father's farm, of the intricacies of animal and plant life. His approach to medicine was, hence, one of finding physical connections before reaching conclusions about causes and effects.

When his studies were done, Galen returned to Pergamon, and was immersed in the work of ministering to injured gladiators. It was a Roman practice that slaves and prisoners were made to engage, in an arena, before bloodthirsty spectators, in violent duels with each other or with wild animals. As gladiators who did not die in the contests could be saved to fight again, the young physician's job was to treat and save grievously injured gladiators. The injuries were unthinkable—torn abdomens, fractured skulls, and limbs that had to be amputated. In those days, the dissection of human cadavers was not allowed and physicians had no direct experience of the internals of the human body. Galen regularly worked with animal carcasses to learn about biological structures and processes. His work in the gladiatorial infirmaries was hence an opportunity to glimpse within the human body, which was otherwise impossible.

In a few years, Galen left Pergamon for the capital city of Rome, where medical practice was crowded with physicians allied to different schools. At first, this newcomer who refused to follow set methods of the trade was resented and shunned. But his spectacular cures where others had failed soon turned the tide and he became well known and successful. His services to the Roman army brought him recognition and State favour and he was able to establish a laboratory for anatomical research, where all kinds of animals, particularly apes, were dissected and the findings recorded.

With well-designed and precise experiments, Galen discerned the existence and functions of many animal organs, and hence of those of humans. His writing was prolific and twenty volumes of his writings, each a thousand pages and representing the first true studies in experimental physiology, are still available. It is remarkable that in those ancient times when technology was hardly developed, there was no knowledge of chemistry and instruments were crude products of blacksmiths, Galen had set out to uncover the mysteries of life.

As a physician with wide experience, he was acutely conscious of the links between different kinds of injury and their effects on other parts of the body. He studied the working of muscles and was able to trace the nerves that controlled them. The names that he gave to some of the muscles in his treatise, *On movement of muscles*, are in use even today.

Through his experience with injuries and what they led to, in the gladiatorial arena and on the battlefield, he was convinced that the control of biological functions lay in the brain and not in the heart, as Aristotle had taught. To verify this conviction, he carried out experiments where he excised particular portions of the brain of animals and noted what bodily functions got affected. He severed the spinal cord between different vertebrae and observed the results, to establish the role of different nerves in the body. He recognized that injury to nerve tissue was irreparable and has recorded the course and reasons for a condition of loss of sensory or motor function in the lower limbs, a condition known today as paraplegia. Even of speech, Galen disproved a long-held belief that it originated from the heart, when he traced the nerves that control the larynx to the brain.

There was a patient who had lost sensation in three fingers of his dominant hand. When Galen learnt, on questioning the patient, that he had recently injured his back in a fall, Galen surmised that the inflammation of the brachial nerve may be the reason for the loss of sensation and prescribed a cold compress. Other physicians ridiculed the diagnosis, as the patient had not lost any mobility of his fingers. But ultimately Galen was proved right, as he knew that the nerves that controlled sensory and motor functions started from different parts of the spinal cord.

In the field of involuntary functions of the body, he was able to identify the kidneys as the source of urine, in place of the bladder, as was generally supposed. Galen also studied the functioning of the heart and came close to discovering the circulation of blood. At the time, it was thought that blood only surged to and fro, propelled by a force of suction exerted by the heart. Galen identified the muscles and valves of the heart as well as the main blood channels. However, he did not see that the blood flowed from the right to the left ventricle, but supposed that it diffused through the separating membrane. Had he seen that there was flow, he may have worked out the circulation through the body and speeded up the developments that followed the discovery of blood circulation by William Harvey fifteen centuries later.

The quantity of new information that Galen was able to garner singlehandedly in his career is indeed impressive. He is said to have written more than four hundred treatises. Although his knowledge of anatomy was based largely on dissection of apes, the volume, *On anatomical preparations*, was a comprehensive textbook that remained the standard source for medical students for over twelve centuries.

After the decline of the Roman Empire, there was cultural and economic decline, the conditions for scholarship in the Western world decayed and the centuries that followed are known as the 'Dark Ages'. Finally, when creativity flowered again, more accurate medical knowledge did arise. These are improvements to Galen's work. The hold that the work of Galen had on the profession, however, was so powerful, that it took years before new findings were accepted.

Leonardo da Vinci

With the fall of the Roman Empire in the fifth century CE, the centre of intellectual activity moved to Constantinople (present day Istanbul), the capital of the Byzantine Empire (or Eastern Roman Empire). And then, for a millennium, till Constantinople fell to the Ottoman Turks in 1453, it was this city that kept alive the legacy of Latin and Greek classical learning. Just a century earlier, a devastating epidemic of bubonic plague in 1347–51, also known as the Black Death, had taken a heavy toll in Europe. When survivors began rebuilding their lives, land boundaries were redrawn and resources became available. There was, hence, an energetic economic revival. This was the time that the scholars and artists who had fled from the Byzantine capital in the fifteenth century arrived in Europe and helped bring about the Renaissance, an era of great artistic and academic creativity.

An icon of this resurgence of art and learning is a personage whose range of accomplishments and interests is unparalleled. He is Leonardo da Vinci, who was born in 1452, in Anchiano, a hamlet near Florence. While he grew to be one of the world's greatest artists, his most important contribution is the vitality that he infused into the pursuit of the sciences. Da Vinci himself is not known for a specific scientific discovery, like a Leonardo theorem or a Leonardo principle, but the energy with which he pursued the idea that nature's secrets were there to find through observation and experiment, and the audacity of his schemes, centuries before their time, set the course of enquiry and objectivity that has been the hallmark of Western science ever since.

When da Vinci was five, his father moved to Vinci, where he spent an unstressed childhood and began to display his remarkable abilities. He showed aptitude in mathematics and was fascinated by insects. He made sketches and kept records of insect specimens that he collected. So detailed and realistic were the drawings that when da Vinci was fifteen, his father apprenticed him to train as an artist. His teacher, Andrea del Verrocchio, a well-known painter, sculptor and metalworker in Florence, encouraged the young da Vinci's curiosity and appetite to discover new things. During the years at Verrocchio's workshop, he not only mastered many kinds of artistic crafts but also sought out and devoured the knowledge imparted by teachers of mathematics, astronomy, botany, masonry, architecture, plumbing and hydraulics.

With remarkable powers of observation, da Vinci had become an authority on the anatomy of flowers and insects, and his ability as a craftsman made him adept with machinery and improving the layout of cities. He was curious to know how things worked and how the ways of nature could be bent to mankind's use. A celebrated area of his interest was in the flight of birds. He purchased caged birds and set them free under controlled conditions, to analyse their technique of flight. As his pursuits were often regarded as outlandish, he noted his observations in mirror writing to limit criticism!

Da Vinci was influenced by Greek ideas and Aristotle's teachings in the physical sciences. As a follower of Aristotle, da Vinci placed reliance on experiment and experience, rather than dogma, and was fascinated by the possibilities of design and inventiveness in mechanics and labour-saving devices. He made use of mathematics and experiment and began to discern how forces worked in mechanical devices, and how even fish used these forces to swim and or birds used them to fly.

After his apprenticeship, da Vinci spent some years with the Painters' Guild in Florence. Apart from working as an artist, he used his engineering skills for public works and even to build military equipment. He had a plan to divert the Arno river, both to provide Florence with water and access to the sea, as well as to deny the same access to the rival state of Pisa. Some years later, da Vinci moved to Milan, where Ludovico Sforza, the ruler, had been impressed by an innovative piece of art by da Vinci—a lute in the shape of a horse's head, with the teeth serving as the keys to choose the tones. At Milan, da Vinci devised many kinds of military equipment for the army and also engaged in civil works. After the plagues of 1484 and 1485, da Vinci redesigned Milan and other cities, with canals for transport, underground sewage disposal and streets whose width was related to the height of buildings on the sides. A famous incident is when a twenty-five-foot clay statue had to be lifted, and da Vinci designed, for the first time, a system of pulleys and lifting jacks, the forerunners of modern material-handling equipment.

Right through these years, da Vinci pursued his many academic interests, including the doctrines of Euclid, geometry, astronomy, botany, geology, and of course, art. His skill in drawing and knowledge of geometry made him a skilled engineer and architect and with his knowledge of mathematics and physics, he devised gears and movements that paralleled the differential transmission in modern automobiles. While at Milan, da Vinci was also taken up with documenting human anatomy and he arranged to be present at several dissections by doctors. The exceptional anatomical drawings that he created were an important contribution to the development and spread of medical knowledge. His drawings of an unborn child in the womb, the heart and vascular system, the sex organs, and skeletal and muscular structures are some of the first that have been made.

This is apart from the 5,000 odd pages of his crafted notebooks, filled with observations, illustrations and ideas of all kinds.

As a military engineer, da Vinci devised a 'repeating' battery, of guns mounted on a rotating triangle, where one set was fired while a second was cooling and the third was being loaded. He devised a tank that carried a turret peeping through a metal canopy, with four wheels, while it was manually propelled by soldiers within the enclosure. He created a diving dome and a manually propelled submarine and even a double-hulled ship, which could survive a cannon strike. However, he did not publish some of these inventions for fear that they would empower the unjust!

The area of research that most strikingly anticipated an invention in later centuries was that of powered flight. With his lifelong observation of the flight of birds, the study of the movement of air, and mathematics, da Vinci arrived at several basic principles of aerodynamics. He designed wings that men could wear to glide or float and even a kind of helicopter, in the form of a helical screw that spun to rise into the air. The sophistication of these designs, at a time when the laws of motion were yet to be formally stated and modern mathematical methods were not known, is nothing short of astounding. It is believed by many that if only there had been a form of power, like the petrol engine of the nineteenth century, da Vinci would have perfected human flight.

All this was achieved by this sole man, in the fifteenth century, when life, even in cities, was still quite primitive. Word of the wonders that he worked, however, did spread through Europe, and though there were many who dismissed his ideas as the ravings of a lunatic, there were others who carried on the baton of observation, scholarship, experiment and discovery, which marked the growth of the sciences in the world for the next six centuries.

Nicolaus Copernicus

We may think everybody knows that it is the earth that goes around the sun and not the other way about. Yes, most people know this today, but people would not have believed this a few centuries ago. Till the fifteenth century CE, the most learned of people believed that the earth was the centre of the universe and the sun, the moon, the stars and the planets went around the earth in perfect circles.

We crossed an important milestone in the understanding of nature when we realized that this was not true. It was this insight that made thinkers look for physical, as opposed to mystical, explanations for the wonders of nature. It helped us understand the change of seasons, and later, how forces bring about movement, and even the nature of gravity.

While the idea about the earth and the sun is now universally accepted, it would not have been easy to work this out on the basis of everyday experience. At this very moment, the earth is hurtling through space, around the sun, at 30 km/second. But the people on earth experience no effects of the movement. We all see that the sun and the stars rise and set, and folktales and holy books tell us that the heavens are the abode of divine beings. All the same, one man, as far back as the fifteenth century—when there were no telescopes, no instruments, and even advanced mathematics was yet to develop—was able to divine from the crude astronomical observations that were possible, that reality was the opposite of what was apparent. The story of Nicolaus Copernicus, who brought this understanding to us, is perhaps the first account of the courage to question a widely accepted idea and to collect data from which the answer to a mystery of nature could be deduced.

Copernicus was born in 1473 in Thorn, a port town in Poland. His father was a business person and civic official, and his uncle, the chief influence in his life, was a bishop and administrator of the church. He, hence, had early exposure to practical sense and this perhaps set the tone of how he thought about the cosmos, later on. The town of Thorn, too, teemed with sailors and visitors from many countries, and this exposed Copernicus to a rich mixture of facts and ideas.

The year 1491, when Copernicus, at eighteen, enrolled in the University of Kraków, was just a year before Christopher Columbus discovered America. It was a time of great commercial activity and the spirit of adventure and discovery. And Kraków was a leading centre of learning, where Copernicus was infused by gifted teachers, particularly of mathematics and astronomy, with a desire to know. In some years, Copernicus moved to Italy and his education continued, with Latin and Greek, Greek philosophy, geometry and Greek and Arab astronomy. In keeping with the tradition of the time, he also learnt painting and made a mark as a poet. He went on to earn a doctorate in law and finally, in deference to his uncle's view that education should be useful to the community, he trained as a physician.

The subject of astronomy, at the time, followed the teachings of Ptolemy (about 100–170 CE), which held that the earth was the centre of the universe and viewed the stars as fixed in spheres that were contained in other spheres. The movement of the planets was considered to be in circles, with epicycles (circles within circles) to account for variations in speed or direction. The system was complex—even ingenious—and, in a manner, had managed to serve the needs of navigation and the church calendar.

Copernicus, however, was not at ease with the contrived Ptolemaic theory of the earth being the centre of the universe, although it had held sway for thirteen centuries. There were alternate conjectures too; the one, for instance, proposed by the Pythagoreans, that the earth, the moon and the sun revolve around a 'central fire'. Also, there was much that these theories did not explain, like the seasons, and the forecasts of star or planet positions, at best, were approximate. Copernicus was uncomfortable with the reliance that the current theory placed on 'humours' or 'caprice'. It was by observation and analysis, he believed, that an explanation could be attempted. In a few years, at age thirty-three, Copernicus quit his position as professor of astronomy in the University of Rome and returned to Frauenburg, in northern Poland, to take over as canon of the church.

Copernicus, with his training as a physician and in the law, was successful in his work with the church and as an administrator. He was active in public affairs and helped the State of Poland with monetary reforms. He even worked as the governor of a province and led men in battle. But all along, he kept up his studies of astronomy and a burning desire to understand. He believed in data and spent long hours in a crude observatory he had constructed in a tower in his mountaintop home.

As astronomical measurements were approximate at the time, the daily calendar, which the church used to plan religious ceremonies, did not keep in step with the length of the year. The Pope, hence, called upon Copernicus, who had become a reputed astronomer, to propose a remedy. The improvements that Copernicus made eventually led to the establishment of the Gregorian calendar in 1582. Copernicus's measurement of the length of the year, at the time, is said to have been off the mark by only twenty-eight seconds.

Over many years, Copernicus made countless observations and measurements and collected massive data of the position of the stars and planets, at all times of the year. Copernicus was then able to discern a pattern and realized that the data just did not fit the Ptolemaic ideas. Copernicus tried out different schemes and finally found that the data did fit the idea that the sun was at the centre and the earth and all other planets went around it in circles. We now know that the paths are not perfect circles, but with the measurements then possible, this was not a relevant detail

Copernicus was excited with the discovery but did not rush to make it public. There was sure to be opposition, both from the community of scientists, who could not get away from ideas that they had long held as correct, and also from the church. Copernicus, hence, held on and collected even more data to confirm whether the predictions of the positions of the planets were borne out after many years. When the results, even of eclipses, repeatedly tallied with theory, Copernicus knew that he had established his discovery quite firmly. It was many years later, in 1539, when Copernicus was sixty-six years of age, that Georg Joachim Rheticus, a German scholar, convinced him to publish his findings. But publishers were chary, at first, of associating with something so radical. The book, *De revolutionibus orbium coelestium* (*Of the revolutions of the celestial spheres*), finally appeared in 1543, but by this time, sadly, Copernicus had started losing his lucidity, and he died soon after.

The book that he left behind was encyclopaedic in its coverage of the night sky. The data clearly showed that the sun was at the centre and the planets went round in circles. The change of seasons was clearly explained, as also was the movement of the planets, which seemed, at times, to move backwards, when seen from the earth. The fact that we see different constellations in the sky from different places and at different times of the year was explained and also for the first time, there was proof that the earth was a sphere.

The book itself was not particularly well received and was reviled by learned men for decades after it was published. But the cold logic of data was undeniable and became the foundation of great discoveries in the following centuries.

Andreas Vesalius

The systematic study of the human body started in the sixteenth century, with the work of Andreas Vesalius, of Brussels. The physician Galen had brought method and science into the practice of medicine in the second century BCE. Galen's information, however, was partial, as it came from the dissection of apes and animals, which was all that was permitted during his time. But his influence was great, and for over a millennium, no efforts were made to find new knowledge. Even obvious discrepancies were either explained as due to changes in the human body since the time of Galen, or blamed on unscientific causes. Vesalius rebelled against dogmatic reliance on authority and brought the progress of medical science back on the rails, through insistence on experiment and first-hand observation.

Vesalius was born in 1514 into a family of medical personalities. His father was apothecary to the emperor, and many others had been in high positions in the medical profession. As it happened, the young Vesalius was fascinated by the dissection of insects and small animals. The practice, since his early days, surely sharpened Vesalius's skill in dissection, which amazed those who watched him in later years. It also gave Vesalius a firm foundation in the appreciation of animal physiology.

After initial years spent with fine teachers and in a home that was full of books, mainly on medicine, Vesalius enrolled in the University of Louvain. Here, he mastered humanities and several classical languages. His passion to study medicine and anatomy, however, was left unsatisfied, as Louvain did not permit the dissection of human corpses. Hence, in 1533, at nineteen years of age, he moved to Paris and began his medical studies under Jacobus Sylvius, a noted and popular teacher of anatomy.

Sylvius turned out to be disappointing. He was a leading practitioner and teacher, no doubt, but of the lucrative, but inaccurate medical system of the age. The manner of lectures on anatomy—a basic science for medical studies—was that a cadaver was crudely split open by a team of barbers, for these were the men used to bloodletting and minor surgery, while the teacher, standing at a distance to stay away from the stench, read out from a centuries-old text by Galen. It is recorded that during one such lecture session, the young Vesalius was disgusted with the inept dissection, while an unconnected part of the text was being read. Many years later, he said, 'The process was a detestable ceremony, where barbers perform the dissection while the professors... from a lofty pulpit, sing like a magpie of things whereof they have no experience'. The young Vesalius leapt up from his seat and took over the dissection from the barbers. Before the professor could stop him, the deft fingers of Vesalius made so clear to the observing students the part of anatomy that was being described, that the performance drew applause and had to be permitted by the resentful professor.

Vesalius, the medical student, grew convinced that there could be no learning of medicine—anatomy in particular—without hands-on experience. He resumed his childhood passion for dissection, experimenting with all kinds of animals, and even human cadavers when he could get them. He often desecrated graves of criminals to exhume the corpse for dissection, and always travelled with the skeleton of a convict who had been hanged, and left hanging for birds to pick the body clean.

After a few years, Vesalius was not able to continue at Paris and he moved to Louvain and Padua, where he completed his medical studies. Soon after graduating, Vesalius was appointed professor in the University of Padua, to teach anatomy. The civic authorities now permitted the dissection of human cadavers and the corpses of executed criminals were handed over to the university. In keeping with his regard for direct experience, Vesalius conducted his lectures with the dissection done by himself, not assistants, and then insisted that the students also carry out the same dissections.

During Vesalius's time, before the invention of refrigeration or preservatives, human bodies had to be dissected as soon as possible. Vesalius also worked on documenting available medical knowledge. Medical practice in Europe then followed the teachings of the ancient Greeks. Arab physicians, however, had done some good work, and Vesalius undertook to translate one of the books by Abū Bakr Muhammad ibn Zakariyyā al-Rāzī, also known as Rhazes, a tenth-century medical savant from Baghdad. Rhazes was a thinker, a prolific writer and a proponent of experimental medicine. Vesalius's translation, made when he was just twenty-three, covered infectious diseases, small pox and measles, the use of minerals and acids, and remedies for a great many diseases, and became an important resource for physicians in Europe for over a century.

While he devoted time and labour to teaching and making demonstrations, Vesalius strongly felt that what was needed was an accurate and comprehensive treatise—a reference work on anatomy. While Galen was regarded an authority, Vesalius realized that Galen's accounts, which were based on the dissection of animals (apes and primates), often differed from what was seen during human dissection. There was, hence, need for an anatomical text based on the dissection of human corpses and written with detailed notes for the guidance and reference of physicians.

While still working at Padua, Vesalius undertook this as his life work, and devoted immense effort in preparing dissections, creating illustrations and writing exact and detailed descriptions, systematically laying bare for the reader the structure of the human bones, organs, muscles, tendons and tissues, in a manner that had not been done before. For the illustrations, Vesalius took the help of the artist Jan van Calcar, a student of Titian, a leading artist of the Italian Renaissance, and known for accurate copies of the works of his master. Calcar spent months with Vesalius, bearing the overpowering stench of the dissection chamber, and created anatomical masterpieces, drawings and plates that embellished the book and have become immortal in their own right. The reference book, *De humani corporis fabrica libri septem* (*On the Fabric of the Human Body*) was published in 1543 in seven volumes; its author just twenty-eight years old.

The revolution that Vesalius brought about in the way physicians thought about the human body did not go unnoticed by the host of traditional healers who anticipated the deterioration of a lucrative market. His old teacher, Sylvius, an admirer of Galen, is said to have been one of Vesalius's main opponents. The result of the opposition was that despite his success, at thirty, Vesalius decided to leave academics and Padua to opt for a position in the Spanish court.

While Vesalius practically dropped out of the vanguard of thinking and research in medicine, the school of students who placed greater reliance on experiment and trial did not decline. His place in Padua was taken by a talented follower, and the break from Galen's teachings, which Vesalius enabled, opened the gates for the many advances in the years that followed.

Tycho Brahe

Science came of age along two main pathways. One was cosmology, or understanding how the earth, the sun and the planets move in their courses. The other was dynamics, or the study of motion, and understanding what makes things move. When details of how planets moved through space and around the sun, nearly in circles, became known, this connected the ideas of mass and gravity, the idea of forces, and how forces act on things. For this discovery, however, the distant and mysterious cosmos had to be observed and measured. This demanded patience as well as the confidence that effort and observation would lead us to understanding. The work of Tycho Brahe of Denmark, who charted the motion of the planets with an extent of accuracy that was unthinkable during his times, is the foundation stone on which modern science has been built.

Born in 1546 at the family seat in southern Sweden, then part of Denmark, Tycho was of aristocratic lineage. The young Tycho received quality education and by the time he was seven, he was proficient in Latin, could fence, write poetry and compose music. At twelve, he joined the University of Copenhagen and studied a variety of subjects, including law and astronomy. The astronomy taught there was of the Aristotelian view, of a fixed earth surrounded by moving planets and unchanging stars. In 1560, when at Copenhagen, there was a solar eclipse, which had been predicted, almost to the day, many years before. This got him deeply interested and his focus turned to astronomy.

The family preference was for Tycho to become a civil

servant. But he was able to convince his uncle, who had taken over his upbringing, and he went on to study at the Lutheran University of Leipzig. During his studies of astronomy, Tycho consistently felt that the knowledge of the time was deficient because the data that was relied on was not accurate. The error of one day in the prediction of the solar eclipse in 1560, he believed, could have been avoided if there had been better data. A conjunction of Jupiter and Saturn, which he observed three years later, convinced him that the data of both Ptolemy as well as Copernicus needed improvement. This drove him to undertake, as a life task, the building up of systematic records of the position of planets and stars, regularly, night after night, and as accurately as possible.

The existing cosmology was based on the findings of the second century BCE Greek astronomer, Claudius Ptolemy, who had constructed an impressive scheme that could largely explain the irregular periodicity of planet movement. The irregularities were explained using epicycles, or circles that the planets described as they went around in larger circles. The scheme was good enough to make approximate predictions of the positions of planets and to guide the calendar of the church. The data that it relied upon, however, was not exact and there were systematic errors, which the more accurate observations in the fifteenth and sixteenth centuries uncovered. Copernicus had made his own observations and reinterpreted much of Ptolemy's data, to show that it was the earth and the planets that moved around the sun. This was both data-based and explained the change of the seasons, and was in keeping with Ptolemy's data. Copernicus's data itself, however, was approximate, at best.

Tycho did agree with Copernicus's conclusion about the planets being in motion around the sun. However, as a devout Christian, he could not accept that the earth too went around the sun. Hence, he devised a scheme where the planets, except the earth, went around the sun, but the sun went round the earth. The scheme worked well enough for many purposes, but still, Tycho, who wished to take nothing for granted, felt that only the most reliable data could reveal the truth.

As a nobleman of means, Tycho was able to pursue his passion, and he did so with intensity. In 1572, a bright new star (now called a supernova) was seen in the constellation Cassiopeia. Tycho made a deep study of this event and his report, which was published, was widely acclaimed. It also broke new ground as it challenged the Aristotelian idea of the stars being 'unchanging'. King Frederick II of Denmark heard of Tycho's work and gifted him the island of Hven as well as a generous endowment, so that he could undertake more elaborate astronomical studies.

Tycho used the grant to create Uranienborg, or the castle of the heavens, a truly sophisticated complex of observation towers, sextants and quadrants to measure the inclination of objects, a laboratory, a library and living quarters for resident and visiting scholars—in all ways a research facility that compares with those created for large research efforts in the modern world. Huge data was collected and special arrangements were made to record and preserve thousands of measurements of the highest accuracy that was possible before there were telescopes. Measurements taken in giant quadrants (one had a radius of fourteen feet!) were accurate to a sixtieth part of a degree (or a thirtieth of the width of the full moon)—ten times better than what had been done before. The paths of planets were followed every night for decades and the positions marked by holes pricked in a brass-sheathed globe.

After twenty years of data collection, there were differences with the successor of the King of Denmark and Tycho moved his establishment, with all his data, to Prague, where Emperor Rudolf II gave him a castle and an observatory. The programme of careful sky watching continued and a generation of students imbibed the discipline of exact observation and observation over an extended period. The path of Saturn, for instance, was recorded for over thirty years. A favourite project was recording the path of Mars, and the accuracy of the data collected amazes contemporary reviewers

While at Prague, Tycho was joined by his gifted student, Johannes Kepler. Tycho recognized that Kepler had the talent and insight to make use of the data that was being accumulated. Kepler was also glad to work with the seasoned master and had great regard for his methods of working and storing data. When Tycho died in 1601, Kepler succeeded his master both in his position as the state astronomer of Prague as well as the custodian of the most extensive and comprehensive astronomical data that could be imagined. And it was on the basis of this data that the secrets of planetary motion were exposed, leading to the formulation of the laws of gravitation and motion, which work together to keep the celestial globes in their paths.

Galileo Galilei

The invention of the telescope transformed the path of science. Till the beginning of the seventeenth century, scientists' efforts to understand nature were based on what was apparent to their unaided senses. Ptolemy, Copernicus, Tycho and even Kepler only knew of the heavens that their bare eyes could see. The entry of the telescope in the early 1600s opened up the skies like never before; much that was new was seen and much of the old conjecture was replaced by fact.

Galileo Galilei, born in Pisa, Italy, in 1564, was a thinker and experimenter, who dispelled misconceptions about motion, speed and acceleration, and laid the ground for their refined understanding. Galileo adapted the telescope, which had been patented in 1608, to point towards the heavens. With its help, he confirmed the Copernican view of the sun-centred cosmos and buried forever the Aristotelian, earth-centred viewpoint. But Galileo, in his lifetime, had to brave severe repression by the church for projecting a scientific finding that, according to clerics, contradicted the Bible.

Galileo was one of seven children, and his father, though not wealthy, was an accomplished musician and a man of learning. Galileo played the lute and the organ, but he was of an academic bent and joined Pisa University at seventeen, to major in medicine. He did not complete his course in medicine for want of funding, but became interested in mathematics and the physical sciences.

It is said that while in the cathedral at Pisa, Galileo noticed that a lamp took the same time to swing, no matter what the extent of the swing. Galileo experimented with lead bobs of different weights and strings of different lengths, and made a remarkable discovery—the time for the swing depended only on the length of the string! This was the principle of the simple pendulum, a device which became the basis of accurate timekeeping in the future.

As a student, Galileo studied the mathematics of Euclid and Archimedes and the works of Aristotle. He was known to question everything and he disputed many accepted principles of natural science, especially many teachings of Aristotle. He had gained the favour of the Duke of Tuscany, a sponsor of artists and non-conformists, and at twenty-five, was given the position of a professor of mathematics in the University of Pisa. Here, young and not as qualified formally as his colleagues, he ruffled many feathers by questioning what the colleagues had long been teaching.

An important matter Galileo questioned was what made things fall towards the earth. Aristotle, seeing that a feather fell slowly, but a stone fell fast, had taught that light things fell more slowly. Galileo could see that this was not true, and we can gauge how strong the influence of Aristotle was, by the fact that Galileo was hard put to convince the scientific community that all objects fell at the same speed if things like air resistance did not interfere. It is said that he once dropped a pair of iron balls of different weights from the Tower of Pisa and showed an assembly of learned persons that they both hit the ground at the same time.

Galileo became interested in how things speeded up as they fell and conducted well-designed experiments. Instead of dropping balls from heights, he devised channels that sloped downwards, where balls rolled or slid down more slowly. In those days, there were no stopwatches to time the motion, but he made do with a kind of water clock: a container with a hole, through which water dripped into a measuring jar. The amount of water that was collected while the balls rolled down the slope measured the time taken.

Galileo collected a great deal of data and came to conclusions that were tantalizingly close to Isaac Newton's laws of motion, discovered much later. For want of the mathematical tools that were developed only later, however, Galileo did not quite get there. He found, for instance, that with bodies falling under the influence of gravity, the distance travelled depends on the square of the time taken. Science students would readily recognize this formula:

$$s = \frac{1}{2} g t^2$$

where 's' is the distance; 'g', the acceleration due to gravity; and 't', the time.

But the representation that Galileo used was geometric, with speed being plotted on one axis and time on the other, to show that speed increased uniformly with time. This was not the more powerful representation in mathematical symbols that was developed later on. His studies on the motion of objects, however, were comprehensive, and most elaborately set the stage for thinkers of the future to deduce the correct relationship, and for great advances in the science of dynamics.

Continued resistance from colleagues in Pisa forced Galileo to leave the university. Fortunately, he managed a good position in the University of Padua. Padua had a freer academic environment and Galileo spent many productive years there. It was here that he got interested in astronomy. Even while at Pisa, Galileo had entered the debate that Copernicus had started by proposing that the earth went round the sun. He showed that motion was relative and the earth could not be considered to be stationary just because our senses made us feel so. And then, when telescopes were developed in the early 1600s, Galileo ground his own lenses and built one of his own, which he turned towards the night sky.

The vista the telescope revealed to Galileo was unimaginable. He found that the surface of the moon had hills and valleys, just like on the earth. He sighted the planets and found that they had no light of their own, like the stars, but were illuminated by the sun. He saw that Venus had phases, like the moon, which showed that it orbited the sun, and not the earth. He discovered the rings of Saturn and four of the moons of Jupiter, as a model of the system of planets orbiting the sun. Where the sun-centred cosmos of Copernicus and Tycho was derived from charts and tables of sightings of planets over weeks and months, here was proof for all to see, that the planets were spherical, and that bodies orbiting other bodies was the norm.

It was about this time that Galileo decided to leave Padua and go back to Pisa. This was a great strategic error. Padua was part of the territory controlled by Venice and there was considerable freedom of thought and expression. Pisa, however, was within the reach of the Inquisition, a process of the Catholic Church to control actions and ideas that contradicted the Holy Bible. The Catholic Church believed that the earth being the centre of all creation was asserted by the Bible. A court of the Inquisition examined some of Galileo's writings that supported the Copernicus theory of the sun being the centre of the known universe, in place of the earth, and forbade Galileo from holding or teaching this heretic idea.

It was Galileo's standing and the influence of his supporters that had helped him get away this lightly and Galileo, for some time, kept his researches to himself. In 1632, however, he published another book, *Dialogo sopra i due massimi sistemi del mondo* (*The Dialogue Concerning the Two Chief World Systems*), a satirical work that demolished the traditional, earth-centric model. This was a serious provocation of the Inquisition and Galileo was summoned again. The only way he could avoid being imprisoned was by publically declaring that what he believed and taught was false and to desist from science thereafter. Galileo was then sixty-eight years of age and had little option. It is said, however, that after he made the declaration that the earth was stationary and the centre of the universe, he added, in an undertone, 'but it moves!'

The voice of Galileo, who led the strongest attack on baseless misconceptions that blocked human minds from seeking the true nature of things, was thus silenced for some time. But the die had been cast; Galileo's writings reached scientists and thinkers everywhere and the fuse of the explosion in science in the following decades had been lit. If this were not enough, six years later, Galileo wrote one more book on motion and mechanics and had it published from Holland.

Galileo never saw this last book, because he had lost the use of his eyes by the time it came out. He died in 1642, aged seventy-eight.

Johannes Kepler

For centuries, sky watchers had noticed patterns in the movement of the planets and had struggled to fit them into a scheme or system. The earliest view, naturally, was that the earth was stationary and, hence, the centre around which revolved the sun and the twinkling bodies of the night. It was a feat of reasoning and honesty, which, when presented with facts, led to the understanding that it was around the sun that even the earth revolved. And, as the circle was the 'perfect figure', it was natural that revolutions, around the earth or the sun, should be in circles. It was basically a correct view of what was happening, but with no suggestion of why it was so.

It was Johannes Kepler, a seeker of order and method in the ways of nature, who deduced from data, that the heavenly bodies, in fact, moved in ovals. He then found remarkable patterns in the way the oval was described, and these were the foundations on which Newton, a century later, laid bare the secret of the movement of the planets.

Kepler was born in 1571 in Weil der Stadt, a small town in southern Germany. His father, a soldier who joined different armies for pay, was rarely there and his mother was not quite mentally balanced. Kepler kept poor health as a child and almost died of smallpox at the age of four. This affected his vision and he may not have been able clearly see the stars and planets whose courses he went on study so deeply. Two events in his childhood had a deep impact on him: one was when his mother took him to see the 'great comet' of 1577, when he was six; and the second, when his father showed him a lunar eclipse, when he was nine.

Despite poor health in his early years, he was a good student and obtained a scholarship that saw him through a theological seminary and then to train as a minister at the Tübingen University. He did not become a clergyman, but proved to be a talented mathematician. He trained in both the Ptolemaic and the Copernican systems, and was convinced by the latter. He was deeply religious and saw in a sun-centred planetary system some theological grounds, apart from scientific justification.

At the age of twenty-three, he was appointed as professor of mathematics and astronomy at Graz, Austria. While teaching the regularity with which the planets moved and came, periodically, one before the other, when seen from the earth, Kepler noticed a peculiar property of the orbits. This was that circles that fit exactly on the inside and the outside of geometrical shapes—the regular polygons—had radii in specific ratios. This he thought, may be a geometric basis of the universe. When this did not work out, he tried the regular three-dimensional solids: the tetrahedron, the cube, the octahedron, the dodecahedron and the icosahedron (with four, six, eight, twelve and twenty faces, respectively), which could fit, one inside another, and describe the orbits of the six known planets (see Figure 5).

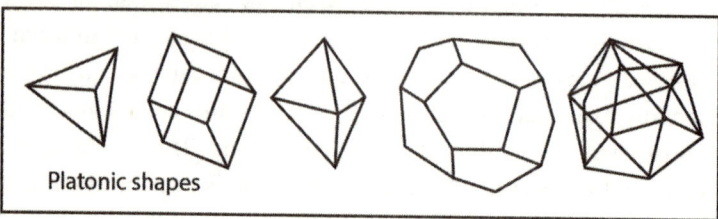

Platonic shapes

Figure 5

The solid shapes in Figure 5 have equal sides and equal angles at all the nodes and the ancients believed that the classical elements were associated with these solids. The shapes had also been studied by mathematicians and Kepler made a valiant attempt to connect their dimensions with the solar system, before he gave it up.

After a few years of creative and not uncontroversial work at Graz, in 1600, Kepler was forced to move out because of differences with the church. Fortunately, he found a position to assist the famous astronomer, Tycho Brahe, the court mathematician to the emperor at Prague. Tycho was at first uncomfortable with the newcomer, who was committed to the ideas of Copernicus. But he soon came to understand Kepler's analytical ability and was happy to share with him his great store of astronomical data. Kepler, too, was ecstatic to work with the master, his instruments, his insistence on precision and his treasure house of data.

Just a year later, Tycho died and Kepler succeeded him as the royal mathematician. And with the position, he had access to the most extensive and accurate record of planetary movements that was available at the time. It was then that he started on his great work of burrowing into the mass of data that he had his hands on, and to draw from it what he had wished to find for so long—the mathematical patterns that the planets followed.

After five years of arduous work, in 1605, he published *Astronomia nova* (*New Astronomy*), the book that contained the first two of his momentous laws of planetary motion. The first law, and the more controversial for the uninitiated, is that the planets moved around the sun not in circles, but in ovals, a shape that mathematicians call the ellipse. Unlike a circle that has a centre, the ellipse is formed around two points, called its foci. Kepler found that the sun was at one focus of the ellipse that any planet described in its orbit.

The second law, of great importance and which guided Newton to work out the law of gravity, was that if a line were drawn from the sun to a planet, the line would sweep out equal areas in equal intervals of time, at all phases of its orbit. Thus, when the planet is near the sun and the line is short, the planet moves fast to cover more area, and when the planet is far, it moves slower, but still sweeps out the same area. This was an exact description of what was actually seen in the path of the planets: that they moved at different speeds at different parts of the orbit (see Figure 6).

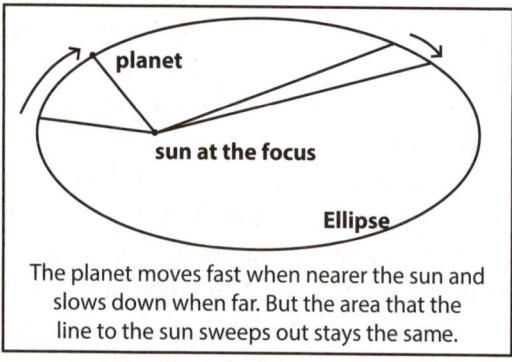

planet

sun at the focus

Ellipse

The planet moves fast when nearer the sun and slows down when far. But the area that the line to the sun sweeps out stays the same.

Figure 6

The finding eloquently suggests that whatever drives the planet must be stronger when it is near the sun than when it is further away. And then, the ellipse was a shape whose mathematical properties were well known. It is remarkable that Kepler, with his poor eyesight, scarcely able to make out the stars at night, had worked out a great secret of the cosmos, just from the data that Tycho had left for him.

Kepler's third law was published in his book *Harmonices Mundi* (*World Harmony*) in 1619. This was a more complex relationship between the time that planets, which were at different distances from the sun, took to go around the sun, and their distance from the sun. The law was that the ratio of the square of the time taken by two planets is the same as the ratio of the cubes of their average distance from the sun.

While these three laws brought out powerfully that there was something mathematical and exact to be discovered about how the planets moved, and perhaps about the universe, the laws of Kepler also moved the study of the cosmos out of the sphere of theology and into that of observation and reason. Copernicus, Tycho, Galileo and even Kepler had to overcome great intellectual and physical hurdles in their work and in communicating their work, but with Kepler spelling it out so exactly that it was the sun-centred cosmos that was correct, there was a palpable reduction in the resistance to thinking about the planets and the stars with the eyes of science rather than religion.

William Harvey

The study of the human body can be said to have come of age when, apart from the parts and structure of the body, we began to understand the way it worked. Till the end of the sixteenth century, although the anatomy of the body had been understood, there was no awareness of relationships among different organs or of how they worked as a system. Each organ was considered to have its 'humour' and 'spirit', and remedies for ailments were prescribed without reasoning or understanding based on a mechanism of action.

That the heartbeat signified life was evident, and the importance of the blood and breath were appreciated. But what roles the heart, blood and lungs played in sustaining life were not known. Medical knowledge was still as Galen had taught many centuries ago. He had believed that blood arose in the liver and was drawn from the liver by the heart. He did believe that blood flowed out to other parts of the body from the heart, but blood was not thought to return to the heart or the liver. The heart was not the pump, but the movement of the blood was thought to be a result of the pulse, a property of the arteries.

The legendary Galen had studied the heart in detail and he saw that blood filled in the right ventricle of the heart and then found itself in the left ventricle. What we know now is that de-oxygenated blood enters the right atrium and is passed on to the right ventricle. From the right ventricle, the blood moves to the lungs, where it gets oxygenated. The oxygenated blood is returned, through the pulmonary vein, to the left atrium and thence to the left ventricle. The left ventricle, which shares a wall with the right ventricle, is a powerful muscle that pumps blood to the rest of the body. Galen did not appreciate that the blood was routed through the lungs and he took it that there were pores in the separation through which the blood could pass into the left ventricle. Here, Galen believed, the blood mixed with air from the lungs, as he considered the pulmonary vein to be an air passage, and then the blood surged up and down the body.

Vesalius, who had made a closer study of the human body, looked hard but found no passages through which the blood could pass from the right to the left ventricle. But he looked no further and only 'marvelled at the activity of the creator of things that blood should sweat from the right ventricle to the left through passages escaping the sight.' The savants of the time had repeatedly dissected the human heart and had seen that there was a passage from the right ventricle to the lungs and that the passage from the lungs to the left auricle was filled with blood, not air. But such was the hold of Galen that facts were distorted so that they did not contradict Galen. An explanation was not sought for the blood found in the vein leading the left auricle and it was explained as caused by accidents in dissection or the shock of death in the person whose body was being dissected!

It was in this clime where physicians viewed the body with awe, rather than to understand, that William Harvey, keen and curious, began to question and experiment. Harvey was born in 1578 in a well-to-do British family and graduated from University of Cambridge at the age of nineteen. He went on to Padua in Italy, where he could receive the best training as a physician. Padua was then the leading academic centre and was teeming with the best minds of the time. Galileo was lecturing there and drew crowds of keen students. Harvey's own teacher was an eminent physician, Hieronymus Fabricius, and the atmosphere in Padua encouraged questioning and creativity.

Medical science, however, was still taught in the tradition of Galen and the ancients, and no explanation was attempted to know what the role and function of the organs were; in any case, not of the heart and lungs. The blood vessels had been identified and traced through the body till they tapered and ended. Fabricius had deeply studied blood vessels and had discovered flaps of tissue—valves—in the larger veins, but their function was still unknown.

Harvey completed his studies with distinction and returned to England in 1602. He trained further as a physician and started private practice. However, questions about the working of the heart persisted in his mind, and he spent long hours undertaking research and experiments. He dissected the vascular systems of different animals, even insects, in the quest to understand. He soon saw the pattern: it was the contraction of the heart that drove the blood down the arteries, and the pulsation of the arteries kept time with the heart.

With meticulous study of the hearts and blood vessels of laboratory animals, he traced the path of blood from the time it entered the heart and was able to see that from the right ventricle, it moved to the lungs and returned to the left auricle and entered the left ventricle to be pumped into the arteries. What was missing was a pathway from the arteries to the veins, to show that there was a circulation of blood. In fact, the blood from the extremities of the arteries passes through fine vessels called capillaries, to nourish body cells. The capillaries then join and reappear as the veins. But in the seventeenth century, the microscope had not been invented and capillaries could not be seen.

Harvey tried another tack to understand what was going on. He measured the quantity of the blood that was pumped by the heart. By measuring the volume pumped out in one contraction, the volume that was pumped out in a minute could be computed from the number of pulse beats in a minute. The volume turned out to be large—indeed, to be more—in half an hour, than all the blood in the body. So where did this blood go, and if it was the liver that produced the blood, could the production be so prolific?

A further tack was to see what the role was of the veins. The volume of blood flowing into the heart was comparable to the volume flowing out. It was also found that pinching a vein led to blood filling up and the vein swelled. And what is more: the blood did not flow back, as the flaps of tissue in the veins were valves that allowed the blood to flow only one way—towards the heart.

Over many years of observation and experiments, Harvey was able to confirm his suspicion that the blood flowed in a closed circle, moving out from the heart down the arteries, and back to the heart through the veins. And while at the heart, the blood was passed though the lungs to be aerated. The mystery had been solved—the heart was the pump that drove the blood to take air from the lungs and carry nutrients to the different parts of the body.

In 1628, Harvey published his findings in the paper, *Exercitatio Anatomica de Motu Cordis et Sanguinis in Animalibus* (*Anatomical Exercise on the Motion of the Heart and Blood in Animals*), detailing a discovery that changed the course of medicine forever. Now, there was a clear purpose to a set of organs, and there was evidence of circulation: that the human body was an organism like a city, with the blood vessels as streets and the blood as goods that moved through the city. These findings led to speculation about how various ailments could be linked to these newly discovered body processes, and medicine took on the character of a science.

René Descartes

Primitive people could represent things and shapes in pictures, like in cave art, but showing quantities—like lengths or numbers, or things that could be measured—in graphical form, was an abstraction that was out of their reach. Our current ability to do this with ease, in the form of graphs, bar charts and pie diagrams, represents an evolution in our understanding of relationships in space and time.

If we wished to convey to others the position, say, of a table that was placed in a room, we could do this by saying how far it was, for instance, from the 'east-facing' wall and the 'south-facing' wall. The position of a chair could also be conveyed in the same way, and our correspondents would know where in the room the table and chair were placed.

René Descartes, born in 1596 in Touraine, France, transformed this simple idea into a powerful method of showing mathematical relationships through drawings on paper. This—the platform for development of mathematics and physics that followed, and now the basis of all science and engineering—was part of Descartes's life work of describing a method of thought to unveil the truth, which he believed was there for the discerning to see.

Descartes kept poor health as a child but was an exceptional student. He quickly mastered the curriculum in the sciences, mathematics, astronomy, history, language, art, logic and ethics, and began to work on his own in geometry and algebra, as developed by Euclid and Arab mathematicians. Also, in deference to his father's wishes, he studied and qualified in law.

Once he was done with his studies in law, however, he decided that it was not in books and reading that the understanding that he was seeking could be found. He then spent, as he puts it, 'the rest of my youth travelling, visiting courts and armies, mixing with people of diverse temperaments and ranks, gathering various experiences, testing myself in the situations which fortune offered me, and at all times reflecting upon whatever came my way so as to derive some profit from it.' In the course of his wanderings, maybe inevitably, he talked mathematics with a leading mathematician of Holland and was drawn back into scholarship, philosophy and the sciences.

He worked on the relationship between algebra and geometry and, along with Cartesian coordinates (as the present system of drawing graphs between two perpendicular lines is called), came up with the whole science of analytical geometry. Greek geometers had found and proved remarkable relationships between lines and shapes. However, Descartes felt that there did not seem to be a system or method by which these proofs were arrived at. He found that representing points in space by a pair of numbers, say, x and y—the distance from a pair of perpendicular lines—allowed the distance between the points, the tilt of the line connecting them and the x and y of any point on that line to be expressed as an algebraic relationship (see Figure 7).

Even curved lines can be represented by algebraic expressions. Conversely, algebraic relationships can be displayed as lines, areas or volumes. Analytical geometry has connected the fields of mathematical analysis and spatial geometry. This has not only enriched both the areas of knowledge but has multiplied, in combination, the researcher's power to analyse and discover. The development of analytical geometry led, in a few decades, to the techniques of calculus, where shapes and rates of growth are related, both to say where a process is headed as well as to work out where a present condition originated. And it is to the method of analytical geometry and its spin-offs in mathematics that we owe all later developments in the sciences.

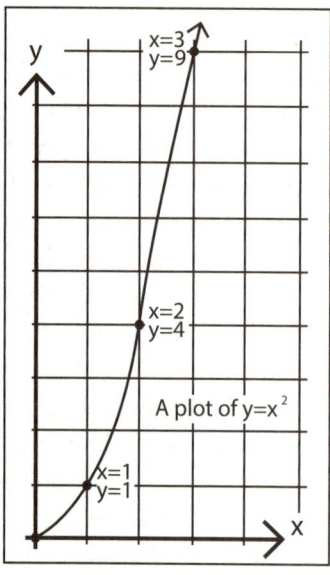

A plot of $y=x^2$

Figure 7

Descartes's specific contribution to science notwithstanding, he is mainly remembered as a philosopher—even the 'father of modern Western philosophy'. During the last twenty years of his life, which he spent in seclusion in rural Holland, he thought and wrote extensively and is credited with bringing in the 'age of rationalism'. His first conclusion was that he exists only because he thinks. 'Cogito ergo sum,' is how it is expressed in Latin, to convey that it is the fact that I think that proves that I exist. Even if I were to doubt it, the fact that I think affirms my existence.

From this, Descartes went on to reject perception, which is often incorrect, and to say that only deduction can be admitted as reliable. He also examined the separation of the mind and the body, which could be translated into the 'substance of a thing and its meaning'. For instance, he says, a thing has substance and it has shape. We cannot think of the substance without thinking of its shape. But if we think of the shape, without considering the substance, we are making an 'abstraction'.

Descartes also examined physiology and psychology. The view at the time was that the human body contained 'animal spirits' that coursed through the body and were the source of emotions. Descartes had no way to change this belief, but he felt the way animal spirits functioned needed to be investigated scientifically. In the case of a reflex action of the body, for instance, Descartes says the heat of a finger touching a hot stove sets animal spirits rushing to the brain and in turn, animal spirits rush to muscles to draw back the finger. This is, hence, an action that takes place without any thought. Descartes believed that the brain itself worked like a machine and with the help of mathematics, the working of the mind itself could be explained.

An implication of this line of thinking was that the human soul itself could be studied by science. If this were so, the soul would no longer be divine. There was also a shift from 'what is true?' to 'of what can I be certain?' This again questioned the authority of the Bible. Descartes's work, although in a place of seclusion and shielded from publicity, was hence regarded as dangerous by the church. This was just the time that Galileo was being baited by the Inquisition for questioning the idea that the earth was the centre of the universe. Hence, for the time, Descartes kept his writings mostly to himself.

Nevertheless, in 1637, he did publish *Discourse on the Method of Rightly Conducting One's Reason and of Seeking Truth in the Sciences*, his work on analytical geometry. The work, of course, was enthusiastically received. In the years that followed, despite resistance condemning Descartes as an 'atheistic threat to the State,' his fame grew and he began to receive royal patronage.

In 1649, Descartes was persuaded to visit Queen Christina of Sweden, to come to the country to set up an academy of science and become her private tutor. According to some reports, it was the queen's schedule of five in the morning, for these lessons, that led to Descartes catching a chill, to which he succumbed in 1650.

Evangelista Torricelli

'We live submerged at the bottom of an ocean of the element air, which, by unquestioned experiments is known to have weight,' wrote Evangelista Torricelli in 1644, when he described his classic demonstration of atmospheric pressure. The demonstration was at once an answer to a question of why there was a limit to how high a pump could raise water and an instrument that has been used ever since to predict the weather. But more than utility, Torricelli's work opened for scientific investigation another area of the ways of nature—the behaviour and the properties of gases and vapours.

Torricelli was born in 1608, and as he showed early promise, he was sent to his uncle, to school in Faenza in northern Italy. He made an impression as a student, and at sixteen, he was sent to Rome to study the sciences. His teacher, Benedetto Castelli, had been a student of Galileo. Hence, apart from the teachings of Ptolemy and the work of Tycho and Kepler, Torricelli was introduced to the work of Galileo. During the following years, till 1641, he worked on many problems of physics and mathematics and followed Galileo's interest in the physics of motion. Torricelli's paper on the 'path of the projectile', a subject that was one part of Galileo's *Dialogues Concerning Two New Sciences*, had been sent to Galileo and was much appreciated.

In fact, Galileo had invited Torricelli to come and work with him, but Torricelli could not go till 1641, when he worked as Galileo's secretary and saw through the editing of the final part of *Dialogues*. The association, though brief (for Galileo died just three months later) was fruitful, as Torricelli had been an old supporter of Galileo and the Copernican theory of planetary motion.

During this short period, Galileo posed to Torricelli a problem that the master had not been able to solve. It was simply that the makers of pumps in the Grand Duchy of Tuscany were not able to build pumps that could lift water from a well to a height of more than 34 ft. The pumps worked by evacuating the space above the level of water, so that water rose to take the place of the air that had been drawn out. This worked well enough in practice, but not when the water column grew to more than 34 ft.

Aristotle had long taught that air was a material thing and had weight. This had been demonstrated several times and Galileo had attempted to measure the weight of air but had gone wrong by a large margin. It had also been shown that if a long tube, which was sealed at one end, were filled with water and overturned, a vacuum would form at the top, with a small part of the water evaporating. But why a column of water, which rose in the pump to fill the vacuum created above it, should not rise above 34 ft could not be understood.

Torricelli's insight was that the column of water rose, not to fill the vacuum created above, but because it was pushed, from below, by the pressure of the tall column of the air in the atmosphere. As there was a vacuum above the water, there was nothing pressing down and, hence, the water moved upwards. However, as the force pushing the water up was only the atmospheric pressure, the column of water could rise only till its weight was equal to the pressure that forced it up. This was the weight of a column of water that was 34-ft tall. Atmospheric pressure could not push up a column of water that was more than 34-ft tall, whatever be the vacuum that was created.

To demonstrate this explanation, Torricelli employed a long tube filled with mercury. He used mercury because it is 13.5-times heavier than water, and the length of a column of mercury, whose weight would equal the pressure of the atmosphere, would be that many times shorter. Italy then had skilful glass workers who could blow a glass tube that was about 40-in long. Torricelli had one end of the tube sealed and filled the tube with mercury. He then blocked the open end with his finger and inverted the other end into a dish filled with mercury.

When the tube was held upright, some of the mercury rushed out of the tube and into the dish, but not all of it. A column, about 30-in high, stayed in the tube. If the tube was tilted, the level of mercury rose in the tube, but the height of the top of the column above the mercury in the dish stayed unchanged. It was clear that what supported the column was the atmospheric pressure on the mercury in the dish and changing the extent of the vacuum in the space above the mercury in the tube, when the tube was tilted, had no effect.

The demonstration of the reality of the weight of the air in the atmosphere was electrifying and affected the study of the behaviour of air and various gases. The apparatus that Torricelli had created, which is now called the barometer, was carried to the top of mountains, where only part of the column of air was above the apparatus. It was seen that the length of the mercury column supported was shorter and, hence, the atmospheric pressure was less. It was also seen that the atmospheric pressure at a place did not stay constant, but changed according to the time of the day, and again, from day to day. It was seen that low atmospheric pressure was soon followed by rain, and that moisture in the air had the effect of lowering the atmospheric pressure. With the coming of the barometer was born the understanding of the air in the atmosphere and the industry of weather forecasting.

Some of Torricelli's other areas of interest included geometry, fluid and projectile motion, infinite number series, mechanics and calculus. A unit of pressure defined as 1/760 of an atmosphere—the 'torr'—is named after him. He was also adept in making lenses and mechanical instruments such as microscopes and telescopes, and earned considerable money selling these. Some of these are engraved with his name and still kept in Florence. A lesser known talent of his was writing comedies. Unfortunately, these have not survived, and we know of their existence only from Torricelli's memoirs, as he died in 1647, at the early age of thirty-nine.

Robert Boyle

There are few areas of modern life that are not affected by the behaviour of air and various gases under pressure. The steam and petrol engines are ready examples, and so is the jet engine, pumps, exhausters, air conditioners, the weather, chemical processes and vast areas of fundamental science.

More than the areas of utility, however, the discovery and description by Robert Boyle, of a basic quality of gases, mark a change of focus in the sciences. After centuries of observation—of the stars, of animals and insects, and of nature in action—followed by contemplation, science moved to active manipulation of matter to test and classify its character. Boyle devised and constructed a sophisticated apparatus to test a specific conjecture, and laid down an essentially exact law that gases follow, and which has guided work in science ever since.

At the time, the nature of matter itself was a subject of controversy. Matter was thought of as composed of the four basic elements: earth, water, air and fire. The Greek thinker Aristotle had taught that matter does not exist without form; that all things arise of substance and gain character when supplemented by attributes or form. Boyle subscribed to a newer concept, the corpuscular: that things were made up of tiny particles that could not be broken down further. This was one of the first steps to let go the idea that matter was a sentient thing with a will or tendencies. Matter could then be understood in terms of the behaviour of the particles of which it was composed. Boyle performed experiments and measurements of weights and volumes when matter changed form, to discover rules that the particles—and, hence, matter—followed.

Boyle was born in Ireland in 1627 into a family of means. He was a brilliant student, proficient in Latin and French as a child. He went to school at Eton College, where he mastered Greek and Hebrew and went on a tour of the continent when he was twelve. When Boyle passed through Italy, he came under the influence of Galileo. He went on to Oxford, and there, he blossomed in the company of other bright students who were fired by the ideas of the philosopher Francis Bacon, who promoted experiment as a means to unearth the truth. The group, at first, had to be discreet in their investigations and called themselves 'The Invisible College'. But this need later disappeared and they were able to obtain a charter from the King of England to form themselves as the Royal Society, the first national scientific society in the world.

Boyle continued at Oxford and established a laboratory and a meeting place for the Royal Society and men of science in his house. Experiments of different kinds were carried out in all areas of science. Boyle was especially interested in the properties of air and Torricelli's work. He arranged for the air to be removed from part of a glass tube and carried out more experiments on the vacuum that was created. For his work, Boyle had engaged his namesake, Robert Hooke, a talented engineer who constructed an arrangement to evacuate the air from a container.

Boyle had found that air could be compressed and when compressed, it could expand with a force—like a compressed spring. He published a book about the physico-mechanical properties of air, which was both appreciated and criticized. One of the critics included Francis Line, a Jesuit priest and scientist known for inventing the magnetic clock. Boyle, in response, referred to a suggestion that had been made: that the volume of a gas depends on the pressure. And to press home his point, Boyle conducted his famous experiment, which led to the celebrated Boyle's law.

To trap a volume of air inside a chamber that could be subjected to pressure, Boyle employed the principle of Torricelli's barometer, but with a difference. In the barometer, a tube, about 40-in long, is sealed at one end and filled with mercury. The open end of the tube is then overturned onto a dish filled with mercury. The mercury in the tube pours out, but only partly. While there is nothing above the mercury in the tube to press down, the atmospheric pressure acting on the dish holds up a 30-in-long column of mercury in the tube.

In Boyle's apparatus, the tube, which is many metres long, is J-shaped. The short end of the tube is sealed. It is then made to stand upright and mercury is poured in from the open end. At first, the mercury settles into a curve at the bottom of the 'J'. But soon, as the mercury rises in the short end of the 'J', the air trapped in the space gets compressed and the mercury cannot rise as high as in the open arm. The difference in the level of mercury in the two arms measures the pressure, and the length of the air column in the short arm measures its volume.

When more mercury is poured in, till the difference in levels is twice what it was at first, it is found that the volume of the air has reduced to half. If the pressure is tripled, the volume falls to a third. If the mercury is withdrawn to reduce the pressure, the volume increases in proportion.

The experiment, which is conducted to show doubters that air was compressible, spelled out a law: of how the volume of air responded to pressure. It was found that if 'P' is the pressure and 'V' is the volume, then the product, P x V, was a constant.

If P increased, V reduced; and if P reduced, V increased.

This experiment with air and the result, Boyle's law, is what Boyle is most well known for. The law expressed a mathematically exact response of a volume of air to pressure and drew the baseline for further research into the nature of gases and the discovery of many principles of matter. Perhaps more important was the philosophical implication. At the time, it was believed that air gave life when it was breathed in; and that it had a life of its own, as it could blow. Boyle's experiment—treating air as something inanimate—implied that the truth lay not in abstract theories but in objective measurement.

Boyle made a range of contributions to science. He measured the speed of sound, and the nature of colour and static electricity. His did extensive work in the mechanics of fluids and conducted experiments with the vacuum pump, including the possibility of preserving food. With his ideas of elements, he could be said to have ushered in the science of chemistry, in a form that was close to the current understanding.

Christiaan Huygens

By the seventeenth century, the scientific investigation of nature had reached a level of some sophistication. The nature of the heavens seemed to be understood, the telescope had been invented, the science of mechanics had progressed, circulation of blood had been discovered, and even rules that were followed by the air and the atmosphere had been discovered.

Christiaan Huygens, from Holland, was fascinated by the telescope and started to think about the nature of light. And he showed prophetic insight when he proposed that light had the nature of a wave, like the waves on water or those of sound.

Huygens was born at The Hague in 1629 in a family of means and influence. He showed great promise as a young student and earned early renown as a mathematician. He became interested in astronomy, and with his all-round competence, he built himself one of the best telescopes of his time. He was skilled in optics and developed a special eyepiece, the Huygens' eyepiece, for the telescope.

Though Galileo had observed the rings of Saturn, he did not understand what they were because of the crudeness of his telescope, and incorrectly labelled them, first as 'moons', and then as 'arms'. However, it was Huygens who discovered that they were actually rings. He also discovered Saturn's moon, Titan, as well as the constellation, Orion. Huygens realized that understanding the movements and distances of the planets would need a more accurate timekeeper than was available. He then used the idea of the pendulum, whose properties had been discovered by Galileo, and devised a clock where the hands moved in step with the swing of the pendulum.

The pendulum clock became a great aid, not only to astronomy but also to other fields, including trade and navigation. As the swing of the pendulum depended on the force of gravity, the pendulum clock was affected when moved to a mountaintop and it could be a way of estimating altitudes. More importantly, Huygens observed that pendulum clocks lost time when moved to places that were near the equator. He had done important work in mechanics and had developed the theory of the forces that act on parts of rotating objects. He explained the time that the pendulum clock loses at the equator was because the rotation of the earth creates a bulge at the equator. This was as good, for a pendulum, as being atop a hill. This discovery was an early geological conclusion at a global scale, which was arrived at from a simple, but related phenomenon.

While still a young man, Huygens had been appointed by King Louis XIV to head science research in France. His work on rotating objects was pathbreaking and is a fundamental part of the science of mechanics. He placed reliance on the mathematical description of physical phenomena and is considered one of the first of the breed of theoretical physicists. While at Paris, he worked with leading personalities in different fields, and befriended the young Gottfried Leibniz, who became one of the world's greatest mathematicians.

One area of great interest was the nature of light. After some years, Huygens went back to Holland and continued his research in optics. He studied the behaviour of light passing through prisms and the spectrum of seven colours, and collaborated with Newton in England. To explain the properties of light, he proposed that light behaved like a wave that slowed down when it entered a medium like water or glass. He explained the splitting of light into different colours by the prism as the differences in the speed of light of different colours when it enters a prism.

He proposed that every point that is struck by a luminous disturbance, itself becomes a source of light. The light then spreads out as a spherical wave from each point and the sum total is a wavefront that is made up of all the waves. The theory was powerful and Huygens was able to explain the laws of reflection and refraction. He used the ideas of frequency and wavelength, first used for sound waves, and he put down his propositions in his book, *Treatise on Light*.

Another area of interest was the speed of light. It was still believed by many that light moved instantaneously from place to place. In 1676, Danish astronomer Ole Rømer found that the timing of the eclipse of a moon of Jupiter, when earth and Jupiter were on the same side of the sun, did not agree with the timing when earth and Jupiter were on opposite sides of the sun. Rømer explained that this happened because of the time that light took to get from Jupiter to earth. This was dramatic proof that light did take time to travel and was support for the Huygens wave theory.

Huygens is best known as the originator of the wave theory of light. With his proficiency in mathematics and the theory of waves in mechanics, he saw that considering light to be a wave was a ready explanation for many of its properties. The mathematical bases of Huygens's theory, as opposed to conjectures of the past or the particulate theory espoused by Newton, was followed up by other scientists in the following years. The phenomena of interference and diffraction discovered soon after, which are effects where light does not move strictly in straight lines, became the final proof of the theory that Huygens had put forward.

Antonie van Leeuwenhoek

The discovery of microbes, made possible after the microscope was invented, opened to our eyes a universe whose existence we had not even suspected. This contrasts with the case of the telescope, which revealed to us details of things that we had been watching for centuries. The telescope showed us massive bodies, some of them larger than the earth, at great distances. But the microscope, in the seventeenth century, showed us things at close quarters—life forms never seen before, of complexity that equalled our own. Hence, the announcement at the time by Antonie van Leeuwenhoek that he had seen teeming hordes of 'beasties' so small that they could not be seen by the naked eye, was surprising, and the Royal Society had to get the claim verified by a high-level committee.

The microscope itself had already been invented in the second half of the sixteenth century. It consisted of a pair of lenses: one the objective, which was placed close to the object to be viewed; and the other, the eyepiece, which magnified the image created by the objective. The early design, which could magnify nine times, was improved by Galileo and then the English scientist, Robert Hooke, and was able to make out details of snowflakes and small insects, like fleas and lice, or cavities in the structure of cork. Finally, it was Leeuwenhoek, a Dutch owner of a drapery store, who improved the magnifying power of the lens used to the extent that it could make out things that were as small as bacteria.

Leeuwenhoek was born in Delft, Holland, in 1632. He first

worked in a general store in Amsterdam and later returned to Delft to start his own drapery store. The quality of textiles depended on the fineness of the yarn used in weaving. In the process of using lenses to examine yarn, Leeuwenhoek became adept at grinding lenses by himself. He also went on to devise arrangements that could image things that were much finer than textile yarn. This was because the power of the lenses that he made was many times greater than those of the commercial lenses that were ground from slabs of glass. Leeuwenhoek's method was to heat and draw a rod of glass into a very fine, hairlike whisker. Now, if an end of such a whisker were melted, the spherical drop that the melt would form would be a very high-quality lens, of a kind which grinding may not have been able to produce. Leeuwenhoek used these lenses to make hundreds of microscopes, which could magnify up to at least 275 times.

Along the way of improving the quality of lenses, Leeuwenhoek got interested in living tissue. He had long started examining all kinds of materials under his lenses—animal hair, skin and tissue, and leaves and wood. Much of what he saw was being seen for the first time by humans and his records show that he systematically surveyed the world of the very small, in a sound, scientifically trained manner. In fact, he soon began to spend more time in perfecting his microscopes and in recording what he saw through them than on his business.

Soon, he began examining fluids. It was now that he made a discovery that he scarcely expected and which startled the world when he announced it. In a drop of water from a stagnant lake, which he placed under his microscope, he saw a colony of moving, living things: thousands of tiny, 'microscopic' life forms; something like insects—with hair, limbs and tails—in rapid motion. Samples of water from different sources like drains and puddles showed similar content of various kinds. So did samples of other materials, saliva, milk and foodstuff.

The existence of minute, invisible life forms had been conjectured, but this was the first time that anything of the kind had been seen. Leeuwenhoek was hard put to get people to believe it. He had been in correspondence with the Royal Society in England, about the lenses and optics that he had created, as well as different kinds of observations he had made. There was, however, some scepticism on the part of conventional scientists when it came to letters from one who had less formal credentials. His letter conveying to the Royal Society that he had seen living, moving 'animalcules', or tiny animals (as he called them), in a sample of pond water was, hence, at first treated with disbelief and dismissed. But Leeuwenhoek persisted, and was able to get the Royal Society to appoint a committee consisting of three heads of the church in Delft and The Hague, a leading English scientist and Fellow of the Royal Society and four others to verify the claim. Finally, in 1677, the Royal Society did acknowledge that Leeuwenhoek had made a momentous discovery.

Fame came rapidly to Leeuwenhoek. Kings and nobility came to visit and glimpse the wonder that he had to show. The single lens microscope as a marvel of technology, used by Leeuwenhoek to image many wonders of nature—microbes, plant and body cells, single-cell creatures, the parts of the cells, spermatozoa, the structure of muscle fibre, red blood corpuscles, and even the capillaries—answered a great question of how the transfer of blood from the arteries to the veins came about. Once Leeuwenhoek had shown the way, equally good lenses were developed by other means and the science of microbiology was launched.

Robert Hooke

Stating a basic law of physics, which forms the basis of the design of nearly all metal structures, devices and products of the modern world, was one of the many acts of one of the brightest figures of the seventeenth century in England. The law is simple and may have been intuitively followed by engineers even before, but it was formally stated, for things to be built with efficacy, safety and economy, by Robert Hooke in 1676.

Hooke was born in the Isle of Wight, off the southern coast of England in 1635. Even in straitened circumstances, he received good schooling, where he excelled, and then went on to Oxford. Nonetheless, he had to work his way through. He did all kinds of odd jobs, including as an artist's apprentice, and developed many skills. All of these made him unique among the scientists of his time, in whose number he is counted as one of the leaders.

At Oxford, he rubbed shoulders with leading men of science and, by necessity, had to lead a life of great industry. His versatile talents were recognized by Robert Boyle and he became the chief support for Boyle in the latter's research work and in running his laboratory. With his intellect and mechanical skills he was instrumental in creating the powerful vacuum pump that Boyle used. Boyle, in recognition of his services, recommended Hooke to be the 'first curator of experiments' at the Royal Society. This was a demanding position, where he had to plan the Society's research, advise its members and make presentations of current science for discussion every week. By then, Hooke had come to be noted for his work on surface tension and the capillary effect—the tendency for liquids to form spherical drops and for some liquids to creep up the sides of a thin tube when the tube was made to stand upright in the liquid.

While he did yeoman work in promoting the research and communications of the Royal Society, he also carried out astronomical studies using telescopes and optics that he had built by himself. The work of Leeuwenhoek and his microscope had been presented to the Society and Hooke was asked to assess its value. Hooke himself constructed compound microscopes and made many observations. His early training with an artist came in handy and his illustrations of anatomical features of insects were published as the book *Micrographia*, in 1664. He noted that the basic units in a sample of cork were shaped like the chambers in a beehive and was the first to use the word 'cell' to describe them.

One of Hooke's good friends from Oxford was Sir Christopher Wren, the architect. In 1666, large parts of London were destroyed in the Great Fire. When Wren was assigned to plan the rebuilding of London, it was Hooke that he hired as his assistant. Hooke is credited with having created a plan to modernize London in many ways, but the plan was not finally approved, as there were vested interests who did not want outright changes.

Hooke was a gifted inventor and through the 1600s, he kept up the pace of innovation with many new devices. One was the dial barometer, which worked not with the traditional column of mercury but with a vacuum chamber that swelled in and out when the pressure increased or decreased. This was a great convenience as the conventional barometer was cumbersome and could not be carried about. Hooke also invented a wind gauge and a device to measure humidity. He could now create maps of air pressure, rainfall and humidity over a region, and started a weather forecast bureau under the Royal Society.

It was in the course of these researches that he discovered the simple relationship of the change in the length of a metal rod or a metal wire when there was a load. He spelt out the law, known as Hooke's Law, that the strain (or the change in dimensions) was directly proportionate to the stress, or the force on the unit cross section of the metallic member. This law now forms the basis for the design of metallic trusses of bridges, the steel reinforcement of concrete, and all kinds of metallic parts and components of machines, from cranes to ships' hulls to aircraft wings—there is scarcely any field of activity where Hooke's Law does not get applied.

In the course of the same studies, Hooke saw that a spring with a weight bobbed up and down at a regular rate, just like the swing of a pendulum. He saw at once that a spiral spring could be used to keep time in a clock and he invented the balance wheel and hair spring. This led to a clock that could be carried to mountaintops or aboard ships that sailed to the equator and would never lose time. It is difficult to estimate the importance of a reliable timekeeper both for commerce and for science.

As an astronomer, he made improvements in telescopes and was the first to formulate planetary motion as a problem in mechanics. He had observed the slowing down of the pendulum clock with the rise in altitude and proposed a theory of gravitation that grew weaker with distance. He studied the nature of combustion and noted that a fire died out after a time in a closed enclosure. He also found that the volume of air was reduced. He surmised that there was a substance (which we now know is oxygen) that was consumed in burning.

While Hooke had a finger in every scientific pie of his times, it is for Hooke's Law that he is known and immortal. But his active participation in all things scientific contributed to the creative clamour of the 1600s and in some or the other way, he helped usher in the great discoveries of that unforgettable century.

Isaac Newton

The brightest jewel in the crown of science was certainly Sir Isaac Newton of England. His two main contributions, the laws of motion and gravitation and the mathematical methods of the calculus, in the seventeenth century, defined the course and gave wings to the progress of all aspects of the physical sciences to follow.

Coming in soon after Copernicus, Kepler and Galileo, Newton integrated into a set of mathematical and physical principles all that his predecessors had observed about bodies in motion, on earth and in the cosmos, and under the effect of gravity. And, building on the work of mathematicians who had gone before, particularly Descartes, he created the methods of differential and integral calculus, the mathematical devices that gave scientists the power to extract the core of a physical state and to simulate its progress, all on paper. The effect of the two sets of tools was that the detailed mechanism of most known phenomena, and new phenomena that were discovered, came within reach of the scientist, and there was unprecedented progress during the next two centuries.

Newton was born in 1642 in a manor in Lincolnshire, England. His father died before he was born and his mother married again, leaving the child to be cared for by his grandmother. At twelve, he was sent to school in a neighbouring county and in the farmhouse where he lived, he was able to play and experiment with interesting mechanical things, like windmills, pumps, models and kites. His guardian also had a library with scientific books and the young Newton developed wide scientific interests and curiosity.

Soon after, his mother was widowed again, and Newton was called back to handle the homestead. But he did not take to the role and soon found himself in academics, at Trinity College in Cambridge. There, Newton excelled in geometry and optics under Isaac Barrow, a gifted professor of mathematics. He also became familiar with the work of past mathematicians, particularly Descartes's algebraic formulation of geometry. While at Cambridge, he also made his first important mathematical work: the extension of the Binomial Theorem, a way to express the result of multiplying an algebraic expression, like (a+b), by itself any number of times.

Soon after, however, the University closed down because the Great Plague of 1665 broke out and Newton returned for some time to his rural home. But in the year or so that he spent there, he came up with the first part of his greatest mathematical work, the differential calculus. This work, which was also developed independently by German mathematician Leibniz, examines the manner in which a value, say speed or weight, varies when we change a factor on which the value depends. In the case of speed, this factor could be time or position and in the case of weight, it could be age, which is also time.

When the values of things that depend on other values are written down in an algebraic form, the methods of calculus allow us to work out the rate at which any one factor changes when other factors change. For example, how the speed of a ball that is thrown up would change as the ball goes up and up. We can see that the ball would slow down and finally stop rising and start falling. Working out when the speed of the ball stops slowing and starts increasing, as it falls, can help us calculate how high it would rise.

In later years, Newton also worked out the opposite of this method of mathematics. This was to take the rate of change of a value with respect to something else and go back to the relationship that exists between the two variable quantities. In the case of the ball, this would amount to working out, from the way the ball behaves, the forces that act on the ball when it is thrown up. We can imagine that applying these methods to the way planets move, in oval paths, when they go around the sun, could lead to an expression of the way the force of gravity acts!

This, of course, was Newton's second and greatest discovery—the laws of motion and the law of gravity, a merging of cosmology and dynamics into a single mathematical framework. Galileo had created a valuable base by analysing how the speed of a falling body changed and had developed geometric devices to show how the body moved faster and faster during its fall. Copernicus had seen that the planets moved in orbits around the sun and that Kepler had proved that their paths were ellipses, moving faster when they were closer to the sun. It was a complex puzzle that Newton had to solve. What he had was a set of facts, a collection of data of how the location and speed of objects on the earth and in outer space changed with time. Could it be that it was the mass of the earth, in the case of the ball tossed up, or that of the sun, when it came to planets, which exerted an attractive force?

The analysis of motion of a falling body by Galileo had been geometric, connecting speed with the distance traversed. The analysis of Kepler, also, was the line drawn from the sun to a planet swept over equal areas in equal time. There was a tantalizing connection, but it took a leap of reasoning to find it. Newton was finally able to see the link. While the speed of Galileo's object, which was attracted by a constant force to the earth, increased steadily with time, in the case of the planet, the speed increased when it was closer to the sun. This feature of the motion fell into place if the force of attraction were considered to fall by the square of its distance from the sun.

Newton now worked out what the force of gravity of the earth needs to be to keep the moon in its orbit and was able to verify that this is the same force with which any object is weighed down on the surface of the earth. He was then able to work out a mathematical proof that the path of the planet around the sun has to be an ellipse and Kepler's observation of 'equal areas swept out in equal times' was a natural consequence.

It was a momentous discovery. Newton summarized the work in the three laws of motion and the law of universal gravitation. The laws led to phenomenal accuracy in charting the motion of the farthest of the planets. Closer home, the laws of motion led to understanding the energy and momentum, the nature of gases and with mathematical refinements, the dynamics of rotating bodies. Even when rewritten to accommodate refinements introduced by the theory of relativity and quantum effects, two centuries later, the basic principles remain.

After some hesitation, Newton published his work in 1684. The three-volume document, *Philosophiae Naturalis Principia Mathematica* (*Mathematical Principles of Natural Philosophy*), when it appeared, banished forever the controversy about the solar system, and became the timeless foundation of the science of mechanics.

Henry Cavendish

The ancient Greek concept of four elements—earth, water, air and fire—being the bases of more complex things in the world, was shared by many civilizations. While different components of the element 'earth' were understood, water, air and fire were still considered basic elements.

In Europe, it was believed that when something was burnt, a material called phlogiston escaped from the combustible substance. Phlogiston was supposed to be absorbed by the element 'air', which was why a thing would not burn if there were no air. The phlogiston in the air was then absorbed by plants. This was why air does not burn and plant matter does. The last element, water, did not support burning, but it was considered a basic substance, like air.

English scientist Henry Cavendish, while researching the nature of burning, discovered a material—a gas—which could be the elusive substance, phlogiston. When this material burned in air, however, the air was partly used up and water was produced! The finding raised questions of whether either air or water were basic elements indeed, or were they parts of matter that were more basic.

Another contribution to science, by Cavendish, was regarding the earth (not the element 'earth', but the planet earth). Cavendish applied the principles of Newton's theory of gravitation and estimated the mass of the earth.

Cavendish was born in 1731, in a rich and distinguished family of the British nobility. After early education in boarding school, he entered Cambridge and then went to London and Paris to study physics and mathematics. His father, a noted scientist himself, had a private laboratory fitted out, where Cavendish spent days and years in study and isolation. His isolation, in fact was legendary, for Cavendish had no social graces and shunned the company of all, except to speak of science and to attend meetings of the Royal Society.

The nature of burning was of scientific interest. The German scientists Johann Becher and Georg Ernst Stahl had proposed that combustible things were made of ash, also called calx, and a substance called phlogiston. Phlogiston escaped when things burned, and left behind the calx. The theory was really not satisfactory, as the calx had been found to weigh more than the original substance, but the theory was current and there was a quest for phlogiston.

Cavendish joined the search and looked in the direction of an 'inflammable air' that had been reported. When pieces of metals, like iron, zinc or tin, were dropped into sulphuric or hydrochloric acid, the mixture gave off an 'air', which was lighter than ordinary air and readily caught fire. Cavendish found that it was the same 'air' that was produced by the reactions of any metal with an acid. It is a mark of Cavendish's skill as an experimentalist that he caught the 'air' in animal bladders, and found the weight of the 'air' to be same in all the cases. He also found that the quantity, but not the quality, of the 'air' produced varied from metal to metal used. It did appear that it was this 'air' that escaped when things burned, and Cavendish concluded that this was phlogiston.

We know, of course, that the gas that acids give off when they react with metals is hydrogen, which is inflammable. But at the time, it was a sensational discovery. The new kind of 'air' became part of all kinds of gimmicks and found application in lighter-than-air balloons, as opposed to the hot air balloons that were known. Cavendish, however, went further. He was aware of the burning of the new 'air' being associated with the formation of 'fog' or 'dew'. By this time, the scientist Joseph Priestly had discovered one more 'air', which was oxygen, by heating the 'red calx', which was the oxide of mercury. Cavendish carried out all kinds of experiments of burning his own new 'air' with different gases, including oxygen. He found that the 'dew' that came from burning the gas that was given off when metals reacted with acids was composed of two parts of this gas and one part of oxygen.

We now know that the dew was water, which is made up of two parts of hydrogen and one part of oxygen. John Dalton's atomic theory, which explains why this is so, was still some years away. Cavendish's findings, too, are better known for the discovery of the new gas, hydrogen, and to show that water was not an element. His discovery of the ratio of the volume of oxygen that it takes to burn hydrogen, however, does strongly suggest the atomic theory.

The other important work of Cavendish was with gravity and the mass of the earth. Newton's Law of Universal Gravitation said that all objects attracted each other with a force that was proportionate to their masses but fell according to the square of the distance between them. This was enough to explain the motion of the planets around the earth. To find out the mass of objects concerned, however, the constant of proportionality was required.

One way of finding this out was by measuring the force of gravitation between known masses. The force itself, between masses that we can practically handle, however, is so minute that its measurement is a formidable task. A workable method was the torsion balance, which the scientist Charles-Augustin de Coulomb had used to measure weak electrical forces. The geologist John Michell had also suggested its use to measure the force of gravity. To Cavendish goes the credit of putting it into action.

The arrangement was of a pair of heavy balls of lead at the ends of a long baton, which was suspended from its middle by a thin fibre, like a silk thread. Next to the two balls at the ends of the baton were placed a pair of much larger lead balls, to attract the smaller balls by gravity. The force is feeble indeed, but the arrangement is so sensitive that the force causes a deflection (see Figure 8).

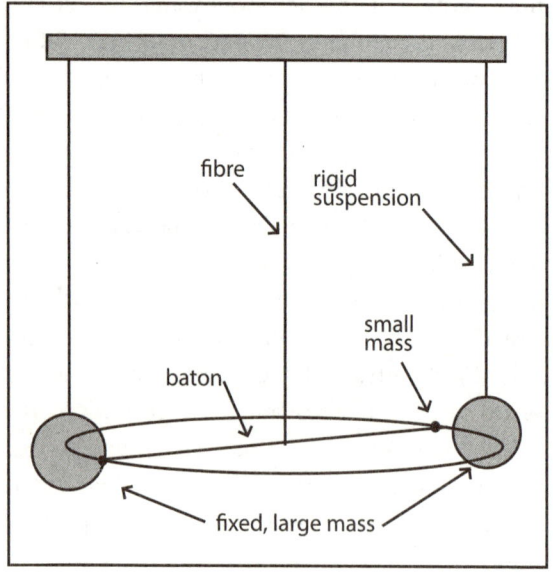

Figure 8

The torsion balance can be calibrated using known forces, so that the angle through which the balance deflects is a measure of the force applied. This, then, becomes the scale for measuring the force of gravitation that causes the deflection. Cavendish used the torsion balance to compare the force by which the balls were attracted with their weight, which is the force of attraction by the earth. As the mass of the larger balls was known, this comparison yielded the mass of the earth. Cavendish derived a mean density, or the mass per cm^3 for the earth at 5.48 g. This is uncannily close to the modern figure—5.5153 g.

Apart from the importance of his two chief achievements, of the discovery of hydrogen and a first estimate of the average density of the earth, Cavendish set the standard for the plan and method of research and laboratory practice.

Joseph Priestley

An important discovery during the eighteenth century was that air was not an 'element', but a mixture of gases. Around the same time that Cavendish discovered hydrogen and the composite nature of water, Joseph Priestley, also from England, discovered different 'kinds' of air, including the gas 'oxygen'.

It was this work of Cavendish, Priestley and later, Antoine-Laurent de Lavoisier, which identified the different gases and components of air, and prepared the ground for Dalton's Atomic Theory.

Priestley was born in 1733 in a village in Leicestershire, England, to a family of Protestant 'dissenters', or a group that had separated from the Church of England. The family was poor, but Priestley was a keen student of many subjects and also mastered several languages. He trained for the ministry and started work as a preacher. In this, he was handicapped, as he stuttered and there was little opportunity, as the congregation at the dissenter churches was not large. To make ends meet, he also taught in a school and gave private lessons. In 1767, at a chapel in Leeds, he encountered Benjamin Franklin, the American scientist. The meeting so impressed him that he took deeply to the study of the sciences. He even wrote a book on the current knowledge of electricity, which led to his being admitted as a member of the Royal Society.

A field of particular interest to Priestley was chemistry. He was intrigued by the odours that emanated from a brewery next to the lodgings where he stayed and he began studying the different gases that were produced in brewing. In the course of his researches, he noted that the gas that came from the vats in the brewery extinguished glowing embers. He also noticed that the gas dissolved in water and the water then took on a sparkle and a tangy taste.

He had, of course, discovered carbon dioxide, which is given off during fermentation, and the sparkling water was nothing but soda. In the same way, he analysed different gases that arose from different sources. By heating common salt with sulphuric acid, he produced a pungent gas, which was hydrogen chloride, which dissolved in water to form hydrochloric acid. Another pungent gas he found was ammonia, which was given off when he heated 'spirits of hartshorn', a liquid obtained from the hooves of some animals. He then sent sparks of electricity through this gas and found that he was able to separate hydrogen and nitrogen!

Priestley was able to isolate these gases with the help of a specific device that he created for their collection. He collected gases, not over a water trough, but through a bath of mercury. If he had passed the gas through water, for collection, many of the gases would have dissolved and been lost. Instead, he bent his glass tube into a trough of mercury and up into an inverted glass jar that was filled with mercury. The gas issuing through the tube then collected at the top of the mercury in the jar.

His discovery of carbon dioxide gas made him known in scientific circles and he was able to quit his duties as a minister of the church and got a good position where he could devote his time to research. He also visited France and met with Lavoisier, who identified the gas 'oxygen', which Priestley was soon to discover.

This discovery, for which he is best known, came through an experiment where he heated the 'red calx of mercury', which is mercuric oxide, and collected the gas that was given off. Priestley had created an apparatus where different substances placed in a flask could be heated by focusing the sun's rays with a large glass lens. Gases that were given off were then passed through his bent glass tube into a trough of mercury and caught in an overturned jar (see Figure 9).

Figure 9

When he carried this out with the red calx of mercury, he found that the gas given off had the property of reigniting a glowing taper! As burning was then considered to be the process of an inflammable material giving off a substance called phlogiston, Priestley named the gas 'dephlogistigated air'.

He found that a candle burned more brightly in this air and even a glowing taper would burst into flame. Small animals lived and flourished in this air and when he inhaled it himself, he felt strong and energetic—properties that we can readily understand today, when we know that the gas was oxygen. Priestley also discovered that plants gave off this same gas, which appeared to be consumed by burning or breathing. If a plant were kept for a few days in a closed container, he found that the air in the container would reignite a glowing taper. Priestley had chanced upon photosynthesis!

It was by then the late eighteenth century and the French Revolution was in progress. Priestley belonged to the 'dissenters', who were liberals and supported the revolution. But when events in France took a bad turn with the excesses of the guillotine, supporters in England were regarded with suspicion. In 1791, a mob attacked Priestley's home and ransacked his laboratory. The Priestley family moved to London, but the resentment followed them and in 1794, the family left England for America.

Priestley was welcomed in America and was offered a seat in the University of Pennsylvania. He was honoured by Benjamin Franklin, Thomas Jefferson and George Washington. Priestley settled down to a home and a laboratory in Northumberland, in Pennsylvania. His notable discovery during the period was of carbon monoxide, formed by heating coal or petroleum with less air. Another discovery was nitrous oxide, or 'laughing gas', which was used as an anaesthetic.

Antoine Lavoisier

Work on gases in the eighteenth century, by Boyle in the physical aspects, and by Cavendish and Priestley in chemical aspects, was rounded off by the work of Antoine Lavoisier, who precisely and quantitatively identified the oxygen gas. Cavendish had showed that water was part hydrogen and part oxygen, and Priestley had isolated oxygen, but it was Lavoisier who showed that it was oxygen that combined with mercury to form the oxide of mercury and the same quantity of oxygen got released when the oxide was heated. Above all, he demonstrated sophisticated experimental technique, which set the science of chemistry on its course.

Antoine-Laurent Lavoisier was born in Paris in 1743. His father was a businessman and landowner, who gave him a good early education and planned for him to study the law. But Lavoisier was interested in science and he studied chemistry, botany, astronomy and mathematics. He had teachers of great ability who imbued in him both the faith in experiment and research as well as a discipline of order and method. At twenty-one, he read a paper before the French Academy of Sciences on the properties of gypsum and two years later, was awarded for a plan on street lighting of Paris, by the king.

Apart from researches in science, Lavoisier did much for civic and social conditions, water supply, hygiene and conditions in hospitals and prisons. In this context, he was part of government councils and much of the funding for his work was from Ferme générale, an institution that took a commission for collecting taxes for the State. While this enabled research for the public good, this association turned against him during the period of terror that reigned in France after the revolution.

A great help that Lavoisier received in his work in science was from his young wife, Marie-Anne Paulze, who translated for him into French the writings of Priestley, Cavendish and many others. She also played a successful hostess at the Lavoisier home to many great men of science, like Priestley, Benjamin Franklin and Pierre-Simon Laplace.

Lavoisier soon had a good position and was able to outfit a laboratory. He believed that accurate measurements were vital for good research and he developed some of the best weighing instruments of his time. Lavoisier then set out to verify and test current theories and conjectures and to put science on solid experimental bases.

One of the current theories, which, in fact, had blocked progress in science because of the respect it commanded, was the phlogiston theory of fire: that inflammable things contained phlogiston, which they gave off when they burned. A serious objection to the theory was that things that burned did not get lighter, as it should be when they lost something, but sometimes got heavier. Lavoisier made careful measurements and carried out an experiment, which is considered a classic in the history of science, to show that the same thing happens when substances form the calx, or are oxidized.

Lavoisier placed a carefully weighed sample of mercury in a retort, and connected the dish to a bell jar placed over a trough of mercury (see Figure 10). The volume of air in the retort and the bell jar was adjusted to be just 50 in^3. The mercury in the retort was then gently heated, and some of the mercury was seen to turn into a red power, the well-known red calx of mercury. As the mercury turned red, the level of mercury in the bell jar was seen to rise, to show that the quantity of air in the arrangement was reducing. This was continued for twelve days, till there was no more change in the mercury and the level in the jar did not rise any further. At this stage, it was found that the volume of the air in the retort and jar had fallen to 40 in^3.

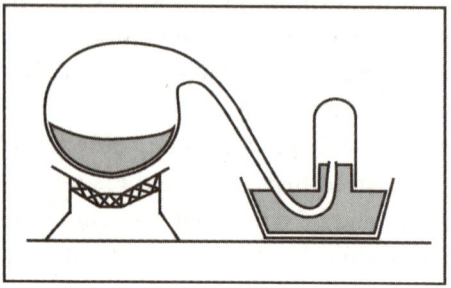

Figure 10

Now, Lavoisier collected the red powder in the retort and heated it strongly, which is known to change the calx (or the oxide) back to mercury. This time, he made an arrangement to measure the air that the calx released. He found that the air released was 10 in^3, the same volume of air that appeared to have been absorbed when the mercury was oxidized!

The experiment showed that just one-fifth (and no more) of the air in the retort combined with the mercury that was heated, to form the red powder—the calx. And again, when the same material was heated strongly, the mercury was restored and the same volume of air was released. It was the same 'dephlogistigated air' that Priestley had made.

Lavoisier also found that the reduced air, when the calx was formed, lacked the capacity of normal air to sustain life, as small animals placed in this air could not stay alive. The air that was given off by the calx when it was heated strongly, on the other hand, was the invigorating air that Priestley had found. The experiment was in effect a repetition of Priestley's, except that it was now done with careful measurements. This important difference gave the death blow to the idea that phlogiston was released when mercury oxidized and it was recognized that with burning, a portion—one-fifth—of the air combined with the substance that burned.

Lavoisier had carried out many more experiments in the field of exact measurements on chemical reactions to demonstrate different features of chemistry, remarkable at a time when the idea of the atomic theory had not been stated. He showed that the diamond, which was known to disappear when heated, was a form of carbon and turned to carbon dioxide gas, the same gas that living things breathed out. He studied laboratory animals and measured the quantity of oxygen they breathed in and the carbon dioxide they breathed out. He also undertook a classification of all chemical reactions and the accounting of the quantities that participated. An important work he undertook was to assign standard names to the known elements; the names, 'hydrogen' and 'oxygen', being two of his creations.

The final years of Lavoisier's life are a sad comment of how social and political events can ignore individuals in its inflamed passion to reform and avenge. The French Revolution was a triumph of courage and independence of thought, which overthrew an unfair and exploitative feudal system and brought in democracy and equality. However, during its last stages, Paris became a bloodbath of executions, with the revolution turning its pent-up anger against all and any as had been associated with the earlier regime. Lavoisier was an icon of commitment to science and service to Frenchmen and the world. He had, however, been part of the establishment and was known to have profited from funds of an organization that helped the monarchy collect taxes. As happened with many who perished in those harsh years of the revolution, this past association of Lavoisier surfaced before good sense could intervene and he fell to the guillotine in 1794.

Joseph-Louis Lagrange

The ideas that Newton had put together were followed up by other scientists and taken to the heights of sophistication. Newton had brought together ideas that were initiated by Copernicus and Galileo and built a framework of how things move as well as the effects of forces. In the course of his work on motion and forces, Newton had also developed a powerful mathematical technique called calculus. With this technique, he could build a mathematical model that worked exactly like the real planets following the laws of motion under the force of the sun's gravity.

Newton had developed calculus in a way to suit the problems of motion that he had before him. At about the same time, the German scientist Gottfried Wilhelm Leibniz had independently created the same method, but with greater mathematical form. Subsequent mathematicians then refined the technique, which became the bedrock of most of the later work in the physical sciences and is today the base training for work in science and engineering.

A milestone in these improvements of the mechanics and mathematics of Newton is the work of Joseph-Louis Lagrange. He was an Italian scientist who spent many years as the director of the Prussian Academy of Science in Berlin and later in France. In 1788, he published a celebrated treatise, *Mécanique analytique* (*Analytical Mechanics*), a work which introduces new concepts of great insight. The outcome was a powerful suite, the Lagrangian formulation of Newton's laws, which enabled solution of problems that were too cumbersome in the ordinary way.

Lagrange, of French descent (his great grandfather was French), was born in Turin, Italy, in 1736. He was training to be a lawyer, but he read a paper by Edmond Halley, the astronomer, and this got him passionately interested in mathematics. He rapidly mastered the field and formed a mathematical society, in the transactions of which are found much of his work of profound importance.

One subject where he made great contribution is the field of differential equations. In this subject, equations contain not the usual expressions in variables—usually called 'x' or 'y', as in algebra—but expressions relating the rate of change of these variables. For instance, the variable of interest could be the position of an object, which could be a distance from a starting point. A differential equation would relate the position, the speed (the rate at which the distance from the starting point changes), and the acceleration (the rate at which the speed changes). This kind of equation cannot be solved by usual algebraic methods and there are special methods to deal with them. The equation could even be complicated by adding terms to account for friction or air resistance, which are variable with speed. Differential equations allow very complex physical situations to be modelled using mathematics.

One of the first applications of calculus is to work out when a thing whose value goes up and down would reach a maximum or a minimum. Take, for instance, a quantity that increases when another quantity increases, so long as the value of the second is small, but begins to fall when the second value becomes large. A formula could be like this:

$$y = 10\,x - x^2$$

Here, as shown in the table in Figure 11, the value of y first rises with the value of x, till it reaches 25, and then falls as the value of x increases. The rise and fall is shown graphically on the right side of the Figure. This behaviour of y can be worked out using calculus, which leads to the result that the value is a maximum when 10 − 2x = 0, which happens when x = 5, as we see in the figure.

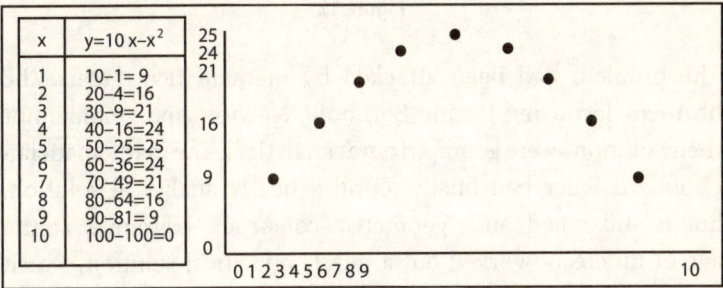

Figure 11

This was a simple example of finding out when an expression has the maximum value. There is yet another area of mathematics where what we look for is not *when* an expression will be a maximum, but *what* the expression should be, so that the value of y should be the highest or the lowest, given the values of x. An example of such a problem could be: what is the path down which a pebble should roll—from a higher point to a lower one; a certain distance to the right or left—so that the time taken is the least. One may think that the answer would be a straight line, but this is not the case. A straight line is the shortest distance, but not the quickest. The correct answer is a very special curve, called a cycloid, and the way to work it out is not at all obvious (see Figure 12).

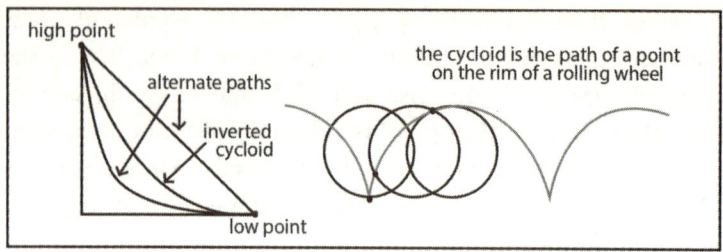

Figure 12

The problem had been attacked by mathematical greats: the brothers, Jacob and Johann Bernoulli, Newton, and Leibniz. But their solutions were geometric, not analytical. The mathematician Leonhard Euler had finally found a nearly analytical solution, but it still relied on a geometric construct. Lagrange, at the age of nineteen, worked out a purely analytical solution, which could be applied to any of this class of problems and merited winsome praise from Euler himself!

Lagrange's method was the start of a new kind of calculus, the calculus of variations, where what one worked with was not functions of variables, but functions of functions. Now, the answer to a problem was not a number, which is what a function yields for a given value of the variable, but another function that behaves in a certain way.

This esoteric formulation was applied to mechanics with great advantage. In place of the normal statement of Newton's laws for solving problems of motion, Lagrange defined another quantity, the difference between the energy of a body arising from its motion and the energy due to its position, like being at a height. Newton's laws were now written in a different form in terms of this new function, which later came to be known as the 'Lagrangian'. In place of the position and mass of a body, to define its state of motion, it was a quantity related to the position and the momentum that were considered. This led to a new formulation that had great advantage in solving problems that were nearly impossible in the usual way. The new way of looking at mechanics also brought to light aspects of mechanics that were not obvious before, and this led to more developments.

While Lagrangian mechanics is the best known of Lagrange's contribution to mechanics, his body of work bristles with achievements in many fields. In astronomy, the problem of two bodies, where one is in orbit around another, had been completely solved. The case of three bodies in gravitational interaction, however, does not admit a solution. Lagrange tackled this problem and made several advances, including the identification of the Lagrange Points, two places along the line joining two of the bodies, where the third body can be stably held by the gravity of the other two. These are the points, around the earth and the moon, for instance, where a satellite can be placed, so that it does not drift!

Alessandro Volta

Although their nature was not understood, electrical effects have been known since long. The ancients, for instance, were aware of shocks that some fish, like the electric eel, could deliver. A much closer approach, however, was when the Greeks observed that a piece of the resin, amber, when rubbed against fur, would attract lightweight articles like bits of cloth or hair. The Greek word for amber is 'elektron', and many centuries later, the same word was used to coin the name, electricity.

In fact, there are two types of electricity. One is the kind that arises when amber rubs against fur and another, when glass rubs against silk. In Philadelphia, Franklin was an early researcher who named the amber kind, 'negative', and the glass kind, 'positive'. Objects that were charged with the same kind of electricity were found to mutually repel while objects that were oppositely charged, mutually attracted (see Figure 13). Devices were also created where plates of selected materials repeatedly moved past each other to generate electric charge.

The Leyden jar was a glass bottle whose insides and outsides were coated with metal and could store a large quantity of electric charge. Charged bits of amber, or the charge in a Leyden jar, could even give rise to sparks. And Benjamin Franklin had shown that rain clouds, which caused flashes of lightning, could be charged with both kinds of electricity.

Today, we know that there are two fundamental charges: the charges of the electron and of the proton. In the normal state, things have equal quantities of the two kinds of charges and they are neutral. Friction, like rubbing, dislodges loosely bound, outer electrons from atoms in a material. In insulators like amber or glass, the excess or shortfall of electrons is not compensated from other parts and the article becomes charged.

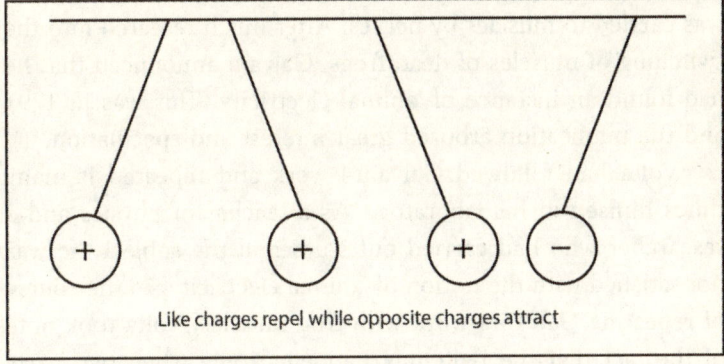

Like charges repel while opposite charges attract

Figure 13

The state of knowledge we have today came to us thanks to the early work of Alessandro Volta. He was born in 1745 and grew up in the town of Como in Northern Italy. In 1779, he was appointed professor of physics at the University of Pavia, where he spent forty successful years. He was proficient in all the electrical knowledge of the time and made a mark with the invention of the electrophorus, a device to generate electric charges. It was a useful accessory for appreciating and teaching the principles of static electricity and the forerunner of high-power machines that came later.

At about the same time, Luigi Galvani, a professor of anatomy in Bologna, in Italy, was working with a dissected frog. Metal instruments had been inserted into the frog's body. Galvani noticed that if external ends of instruments of dissimilar metals were to touch, the frog's leg would twitch. He repeated the action with probes of different metals and found that all dissimilar pairs had the same effect. It was known at the time that contact with electrically charged objects caused a twitch in animal muscles, as a 'shock'. It was also believed that muscular activity itself was because of an 'electric fluid' that was carried to muscles by nerves. After much research into the twitching of muscles of dead frogs, Galvani announced that he had found an instance of 'animal electricity'. This was in 1791 and the publication aroused great interest and speculation.

Volta had followed Galvani's work and repeated it many times himself in his laboratory. As a teacher of physics and a researcher who had carried out studies in the subject, he was not satisfied with the notion of 'animal electricity'. In the course of repeating Galvani's work with frog muscles, Volta took note of the fact that the twitching happened only when two parts of the muscle were connected by metal, and again, only where different metals were involved. He reasoned that the source was not something in the muscles that was activated when connected by metal, but the twitching arose from the fact that there were two metals.

His researches had also examined the effect of electricity on the senses of touch, taste and sight. He now decided to carry out an experiment on himself: of monitoring, by sensation, the effect that dissimilar metals had. He placed a coin of gold on his tongue and one of silver under his tongue. When he connected the two coins with a metal wire, he did not feel a twitch, but he did observe a sour taste. He still thought it was an instance of animal electricity emerging from his tongue. But he continued his experiments, and in 1796, he discovered there could be electric effects even when there was a piece of card that had been soaked in salty water, in place of his tongue, between the coins!

Volta continued his researches and experimented with different metals. In 1799, he perfected the Voltaic pile, a stack of alternating discs of copper and zinc, separated by a brine-soaked card. When the bottom disc was connected to the uppermost disc with a wire, there was a continuous current of electricity. His letter, in 1800, to the Royal Society, was a sensation the world over. It debunked the idea that electricity was generated by living things and proved that it could be produced by metals and through chemical means.

The idea was grabbed by researchers in all fields and new results were rapidly reported. Electrolysis (the dissociation of substances like water into hydrogen and oxygen), or the extraction of metals from solutions with the help of electricity, was developed. As a continuous electric current was now possible, the magnetic effects of electric currents and the electric motor were discovered. The field of electromagnetism was opened and the many wonders of the modern world rapidly followed.

What also followed was admiration and adulation. In 1801 in Paris, Volta gave a demonstration of his battery generating electric current before Napoleon, who made him a count and a senator. The Austrian emperor also made him director of the philosophical faculty at the University of Padua. In 1881, the volt—the unit of the electromotive force that drives current—was named after him.

Edward Jenner

By the end of the eighteenth century, there was considerable knowledge of anatomy and a glossary of diseases, symptoms and remedies. Understanding of the mechanism of body processes and the trail of cause-and-effect in a disease and its cure, however, had to wait until much later. The germ theory of disease was only a conjecture and the practice of medicine still followed the miasma theory, a belief that there was 'bad air' emanating from diseased tissue. Edward Jenner's discovery of a positive and definite procedure to impart immunity against one of the most fearful diseases of the time marks the beginning of a scientific view of disease.

Small pox, known since ancient times, became a great threat with the growth of cities. It is estimated that by the end of the eighteenth century, Europe saw 400,000 deaths from smallpox every year. The disease itself causes great discomfort, with large parts of the body covered by pustules, which ooze pus, and give off a powerful stench. About a quarter of the persons infected during an epidemic did not survive and those that did were left disfigured with scars on the face. Many went blind.

A remarkable feature about the disease, however, was that those who had survived an attack were immune thereafter. This fact had been exploited in Eastern countries, where a mild form of smallpox was induced in healthy persons. The practice, of course, had the risk that the person would develop full-fledged smallpox and was only sparingly used in Europe. Another interesting fact was that persons (often milkmaids), who had contracted a mild rash with fever, called cowpox, also never came down with smallpox. People, however, were so much in dread of smallpox, plague and other scourges of the times, that it did not cross anybody's mind that this pattern may be of importance.

Jenner was born in 1749 in Gloucestershire, southwest England. Young Edward became interested in biology and went on to study medicine. His early training was with capable doctors, and at the age of twenty-one, he went to London to work at St George's Hospital, with Dr John Hunter. Dr Hunter was a man with great imagination and enthusiasm, who believed in following clues and trying things out. Apart from learning well in medical skills, Jenner picked up from Dr Hunter the important trait of looking for connections and discovering through experiments.

When his medical studies were over, Jenner went back to Gloucestershire and set up practice. In the course of his practice over many years, he came across all kinds of disease and noted that there were all kinds of substances and folk knowledge that were used to cure or prevent disease. That moulds, which were later found to contain penicillin, could cure infections was known and so were many other home remedies. It was also known that an attack of measles conferred immunity. It was, hence, a good thing if a girl caught it in childhood, for the disease was dangerous in a grown woman. An interesting thing in rural Gloucestershire was that milkmaids, who had caught cowpox, were immune to smallpox.

While this connection between cowpox and smallpox was generally known, Jenner felt this was something to follow up systematically. Hence, he began to carefully document the instances of cowpox and smallpox that came before him. He could soon assert, with documentary proof, that an exposure to cowpox was a definite protection against smallpox, even if the person came into close contact with a smallpox patient. In a historic demonstration, he first infected James Phipps, his gardener's eight-year-old son, with cowpox from the blisters of Sarah Nelmes, a milkmaid who had caught cowpox from a cow called Blossom. The boy developed mild symptoms and soon was well. Next, Jenner injected Phipps with scab material from a smallpox patient, a weakened infection. This was a method of inducing immunity that was often followed. While it was not without the danger of a serious attack of smallpox, it normally induced a mild form, from which the patient recovered and was immune thereafter.

Phipps, however, developed no symptoms of smallpox. Even when the injection of smallpox material was repeated, he remained well. This was a dramatic demonstration that infection with cowpox was protection against smallpox—not just cowpox from the cow, but also the cowpox material from a person infected with cowpox. In his methodical way, Jenner carried out the same trial with many other persons and when he was satisfied, he published his findings in 1796.

The news of the discovery spread fast and far. The practice of vaccination spread all over Europe and was exported to the Americas, Philippines, Macao and China. Napoleon, who was at war with England, had his troops vaccinated and at Jenner's request, released all English prisoners of war, as he could 'refuse nothing to one of the greatest benefactors of mankind.' It is said that Jenner's discovery has saved more lives than any other action in the world. In England, he was awarded a generous pension so that he could work full-time in the field of vaccination. He was appointed physician to the King and made Mayor of his birthplace, Berkley.

Vaccination was soon taken up as a mission by states and

governments and there was rapid reduction in the number of new cases. Total eradication took a long time, but the terror that smallpox had created in past decades was soon forgotten. Perhaps more important than the relief from smallpox is the concept of vaccination and the spirit of finding scientific answers that Jenner's discovery created. That disease came from infection, and that the body had an immune system was soon realized. Vaccines against more infections were discovered and medical science, like the physical sciences, joined the march towards modernity.

Count Rumford

Heat—which is now understood as a form of motion of the atom-scale components of things—was earlier imagined to be a kind of fluid, called 'caloric', which flowed in and out of bodies to cause heating or cooling. The first steps in dispelling this notion were taken by Benjamin Thompson, who moved from the then recently formed USA to Europe, where he was made a count by the Bavarian Court.

Thompson was born in 1753 in a small town in Massachusetts. He went to the village school but often visited the nearby Harvard College in Cambridge, to attend lectures. He was fascinated by perpetual motion machines and took interest in eclipses. At the age of eighteen, he became a schoolmaster in the town of Rumford in Massachusetts and got a position in the New Hampshire Militia. He appears to have been a British loyalist during the American civil war and used devices like invisible ink in espionage activities.

He was, however, a scientist at heart and carried out lunar observations, experiments on the speed of projectiles fired by cannons and the properties of gunpowder. By the time he left for England, which was a few years later, he already had a reputation as a scientist, and was soon elected a Fellow of the Royal Society. After some years in England, he migrated to Bavaria, where he rose to a high position in the court and the military. He spent eleven years in Bavaria, applying his talents in reorganizing the army and the administration of the state. It was during this period, while working in the foundries that bored the barrels of the cannon, that he made observations that ran counter to the current theory of heat.

Heat, at the time, was considered to be an aether called 'caloric', which flowed in and out of materials. Caloric was considered to be indestructible and incapable of being created, perhaps the last of the Aristotelian ideas of the four essences of matter—earth, air, water and fire. The word 'caloric', for the essence of heat, had been coined by Lavoisier, the French chemist who had showed that mercury got heavier, not lighter, when burned.

Thompson was able to see that energy was expended in driving the bit that bored the barrels, which in turn grew so hot that they could keep the cooling water boiling continuously. The conclusion was not difficult to reach, that the heat came from mechanical work, not any currents of caloric! In 1798, Thompson published his work as 'An Experimental Enquiry Concerning the Source of the Heat which is Excited by Friction', in the *Philosophical Transactions of the Royal Society*. This was the start of a scientific look at heat and work, which led to the kinetic theory, the laws of thermodynamics, the steam engine and the petrol engine!

Thompson made important contributions to the administration of the Bavarian state and brought the scientific method to dealing with civic problems. One area was of engaging the impoverished peasant population of the country in paid work, by getting them to make uniforms for the army, which was itself low in morale. He developed a specially formulated 'soup' that was economical and nutritious and was served both in the army and in the workhouses. This may be considered one of the earliest scientific steps in the domain of dietetics. The Bavarian State recognized his services and he was made a count. As his title, he took the name of his hometown, as Count Rumford.

Count Rumford went on to be celebrated for many inventions, including the double boiler, a kitchen range, the pressure cooker, the folding bed and important improvements that he made in the design of fireplaces. In 1796 and 1798, he wrote two papers detailing the improved design of the fireplace, which were widely read, and in the 1790s, the 'Rumford fireplace' became a state-of-the-art technology worldwide. In a few years, Count Rumford left Bavaria for England and France, and was as successful in science and commerce and as in the arts and the social sphere. In 1796, he gave $5,000 each to the Royal Society of Great Britain and to the American Academy of Arts and Sciences to award medals every two years for outstanding scientific research on heat or light. When he died, most of his considerable fortune went to Harvard University.

But even if there were no other contributions to science, Count Rumford would be immortal for his invention of the 'drip-pot coffee percolator'. This is the simple arrangement of two containers, one above the other, with the base of the upper one pierced with little holes. Pure coffee powder is packed in the upper container and covered with boiling water. The water drips into the lower container, as the aromatic decoction! (See Figure 14).

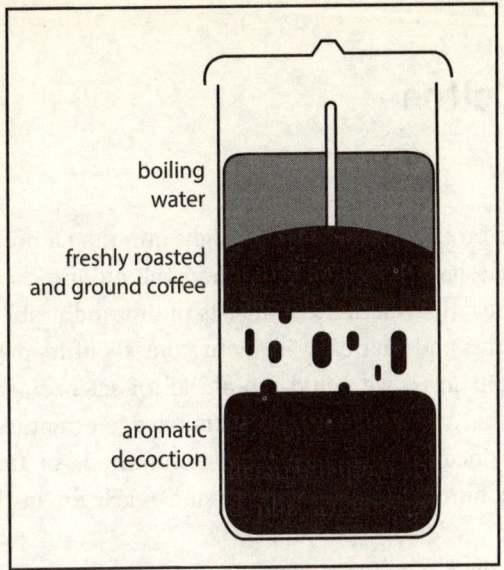

boiling
water

freshly roasted
and ground coffee

aromatic
decoction

Figure 14

John Dalton

There is probably no piece of insight into the nature of matter that has had greater impact than the atomic theory. With this one idea, that 'all matter consists of tiny, indivisible particles called atoms, and that each element consists of its own kind of identical particles', we could rebuild all of science as we know it. This is because the amount of knowledge of nature that has collected since the atomic theory is hundreds of times more than what humanity had to grope and reach for in the earlier centuries.

There, had, of course, been the concept of matter consisting of indivisible particles, at least in the ancient Greek and Indian civilizations. These assertions, however, were philosophical conjectures and not a framework based on evidence and experiment, to explain other, documented physical phenomena. The atomic theory, spelt out by John Dalton, on the other hand, is built on factual data, mainly about the composition of air and the behaviour of gases, and proposes a mechanism to explain them.

Dalton was born in 1766 in Eaglesfield, a village in northern England. He was a prodigy, and as a child, he learnt Latin and Greek on his own and excelled in mathematics. He was permitted, at the age of twelve, to open his own school. At fifteen, he moved to Kendal, a nearby town, again as a teacher. He continued to learn science and mathematics, and kept a daily record of the weather, a practice that he kept up all his life.

After twelve years at Kendal, Dalton became a teacher in

Manchester, an industrial town, where there was lively interest in and discussion of the sciences. The meteorological observation that he had published got recognition and he became an active member of Manchester's Literary and Philosophical Society. He continued his researches on the weather and made several presentations before the Society.

It was in the course of his study of the atmosphere that he was drawn into the study of gases and then the ratios in which gases combined. Boyle had discovered that air had a 'spring', or exerted pressure, and resisted being compressed. Cavendish, Priestley and Lavoisier had shown that air consisted of different gases and even water was made up of two of them. At the time it was not clear how a body of one gas could merge with that of another gas. Dalton, in his study of gases, found that if a quantity of nitrogen in a container exerted a certain pressure and a quantity of oxygen in that container exerted a certain pressure, then the two gases together exerted the sum of the pressures they exerted separately.

This observation, now known as Dalton's Law of Partial Pressures, suggested to him that the two gases could mingle, like groups of people in a room. In the course of his meteorological studies, he had collected samples of air from far and near, mountaintops, the countryside and sooty Manchester. He found that all the samples contained the gases, nitrogen, oxygen, carbon dioxide and water vapour, in nearly the same proportions. He carried out an experiment where he placed a jar of hydrogen face down on a jar of carbon dioxide. It would be expected that hydrogen would stay on top and the heavier carbon dioxide would remain below. But no; the gases soon mixed and were in the same proportions at any part of the two jars. And again, if a bottle of a volatile substance were opened at one end of a room, the smell soon permeated all over.

The conclusion had to be that gases were 'porous': they allowed other gases to pass through, as if each gas occupied the whole container. The model that suggested itself was that gases consisted of minute particles separated by large distances, in comparison to their own dimensions. The word Dalton chose to describe the particles was 'atoms', from the word 'atomos', meaning 'uncut', that the Greeks had used to describe the ultimate, indivisible elements of matter.

Other experiments that Dalton carried out were with gases that combined. He found that oxygen would combine, in closed vessels over water, with either one volume of nitrous oxide or with two volumes. To be specific, the oxygen to nitrogen ratio in the two gases, nitrous oxide and nitrous gas (which we now call nitric oxide), is 0.58 and 1.27. We can see that the two ratios are very nearly whole number multiples. There is a similar relationship with the oxides of carbon, when carbon burns to form carbon dioxide or when it burns in restricted air to form carbon monoxide. This proportionality—that elements combine in whole number ratios—strongly suggested that the atoms of the elements combine in simple whole number ratios.

Dalton then used available data on the weights of different elements of which compounds were formed to estimate the ratios of the weight of atoms. He set the weight of the hydrogen atom as '1' and that of other atoms as multiples—known as 'atomic weights'—of the weight of the hydrogen atom. Lavoisier had found that 85 per cent oxygen, by weight, combines with 15 per cent, by weight, of hydrogen. This put the weight of oxygen about six times that of hydrogen. Dalton took the numbers to be 7 and 1 and placed the atomic weight of oxygen at 7. We now know that an atom of oxygen combines not with one but two atoms of hydrogen. And the ratio is 8, rather than 7, which puts the atomic weight of oxygen at 16. But Dalton had made a start, and like oxygen, he estimated the atomic weights of many other elements.

The chemical industry had made some progress by then and many products were created by mixing components in proportions that were known to work. The knowledge of atomic weights brought mathematical exactness and understanding to these processes. The practices of grinding and mixing were transformed into a science. The atomic theory was rapidly accepted by the scientific community. Dalton was honoured by the French Academy of Sciences and the Royal Society. Research was undertaken with new purpose, to detect and measure the properties of invisible atoms, which revealed themselves in the bulk properties of matter. The idea of the atom entered all work in science and has dominated ever since.

André-Marie Ampère

Magnetism was perhaps the first 'higher science' phenomenon that early humans became aware of. They learnt that bits of loadstone (the mineral magnetite, an oxide of iron) would stick together and attract pieces of iron. Around the twelfth century, it was known that a bit of loadstone that was free to move would point to the north, a property that was useful in navigation.

Of electricity, it was known that materials like amber or glass, when they rub against cloth, attract bits of fluff or feathers. The electric charge was discovered only in the seventeenth century and the electric current, only in the eighteenth century.

There was, however, no suggestion or suspicion that electricity (which arose in fragile things like amber and glass) and magnetism (which was found in stones and iron) could be related.

With the discovery of the Voltaic cell in 1800, the electric current became a phenomenon of intense study. One of the first applications of electric current was in the decomposition of water into hydrogen and oxygen, which led to progress in chemistry. The resistance that conductors offered to electric current and the heating effect of the current were also soon discovered. But in 1820, a new observation by the Dane, Hans Christian Ørsted, was that a wire carrying an electric current would turn the direction of a magnetic needle.

The magnetic needle was a magnetized piece of iron mounted in a way that it could swing freely from side to side.

The needle settles down in a north-south (N-S) direction. Ørsted found that if there was an electric wire alongside, the needle turned its direction every time the current was switched on. The usual N-S alignment of the magnetic needle was thought to be because the earth itself, with its magnetic ores, was magnetized. But it was startling to find that a wire with an electric current could affect a magnet. When Ørsted's discovery was announced, it spurred the scientific community to instant activity.

André-Marie Ampère, professor of analytical mathematics and mechanics at École Polytechnique, in Paris, was among the first to react. Within a week of the announcement, Ampère, an accomplished scientist and mathematician, repeated Ørsted's experiment, but with meticulous controls. While Ørsted had observed an effect in certain conditions, Ampère went further and carried out measurements of the magnetic effect of the current in the wire. He set up a pair of parallel conductors, one fixed, and the other free to move. He found that when a current passed through the two conductors in the same direction, the free conductor was drawn towards the other, but when the current was in opposing directions, the conductor was repelled.

This was a finding with two conductors carrying currents (just the conductors, with no loadstone or a magnetic needle in the picture). It showed that each current-carrying conductor behaved like the magnetic needle, or a magnet. It may appear that this was not a difficult thing to reason out, once Ørsted's discovery was announced. But in fact, it was not obvious at the time. On why Ørsted had not experimented with wires carrying currents, Ampère suggested an explanation. While a bar of soft iron has the effect of deflecting a magnetic needle, a bar of soft iron has no effect on another bar of iron. So also, a current-carrying wire that affects a magnetic needle need not (at least, not obviously) affect another current-carrying wire, Ampère suggested (see Figure 15).

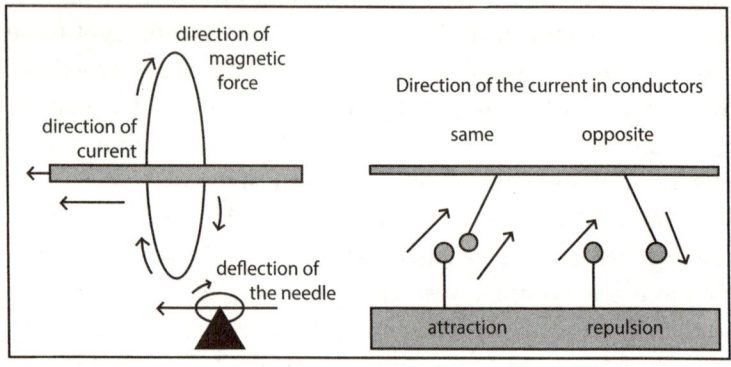

direction of magnetic force

direction of current

deflection of the needle

Direction of the current in conductors

same   opposite

attraction   repulsion

Figure 15

Ampère was born in Lyons in 1775, the son of a prosperous merchant. His father was a man of learning and participated in young Ampère's academic growth, encouraging him to learn Latin and Greek. But Ampère was inclined towards the sciences. He showed great ability in mathematics and was proficient in calculus by the time he was twelve. The violence and excesses in France after the revolution, however, overtook the Ampères, and Ampère senior, suspected of being a loyalist, was put to the guillotine. Ampère was shattered. In a year, fortunately, he recovered and continued his studies, while also working as a tutor to make ends meet.

A little later, after he was married and blessed with a son, he moved on as a science professor in a government school in Bourg-en-Bresse, to the north of Lyons. Here, he continued the researches he had begun in many fields and published a paper on the subject of chance and probability, which caught the attention of senior mathematicians. His progress, however, was again disturbed when he lost his wife and became distraught. Fortunately, Napoleon Bonaparte arranged for a position in Ècole Polytechnique in Paris, which Ampère accepted.

It was because of Ampère's immersion in many fields of science that he was perfectly prepared, when Ørsted announced his observation, to follow through with an experiment that converted the latter's observation into a principle of electromagnetism with far-reaching implications. After the epochal demonstration with two conductors, he continued to measure and map the magnetic force around a conductor, and found that it acted symmetrically in circles around the conductor and got weaker as one moved away from the conductor. The direction of the force, along the circles, also depended on the direction of the current in the conductor. This explained both the effect the current had on the magnetic needle as well as the attraction and repulsion of the parallel conductors.

Ampère went further and developed a mathematical expression for the direction and the strength of the magnetic force exerted by a given current flowing in a straight wire or circular loop. The exact mathematical formula gave wings to research in electromagnetism, led to the marvel of the electric motor and is the basis of design in electrical engineering to this day.

He next turned to coils of wires that carried electricity, and found that a coil, called a solenoid, behaved as if it were a real magnet, with a pole at each end. He found that placing a bar of iron inside a solenoid with a current was a method to create a strong bar magnet.

From these magnetic effects of electric currents, Ampère suggested that the magnetism of iron oxides or magnets themselves may arise from electric currents within the atoms of iron. This was a conclusion of his seminal theory, published in 1803. To suggest that the magnetism of atoms may come from electricity was prophetic. It was seventy years later that the electron, the particle that carries electric charge, was found to be part of the atom, and the nature of magnetism was found to be as Ampère had imagined.

The discovery and the theoretical construct that was built by him became the rock foundation for breathtaking progress in the theory and application of electricity and magnetism in the following century. The unit for the measurement of electric current—the ampere—was rightly named after him.

Thomas Young

A spectacular demonstration of the wave theory of light is the Young's two-slit experiment, which was specifically fashioned by a veritable genius and polymath, the breadth of whose knowledge and accomplishments astounded alike his contemporaries and the scholars who came after. This was Thomas Young, born in 1773 in a little village in southwest England, who went onto make important contributions to optics, mechanics, mathematics, physiology, medicine, music, languages and Egyptology. By the time he was fourteen, he had learnt Greek and Latin and was acquainted with French, Italian, Hebrew, German, Aramaic, Syriac, Samaritan, Arabic, Persian, Turkish and Amharic!

Young trained as a physician, qualifying as a doctor of medicine, and established practice in London. His interests, however, were wide and he carried out research in many fields. In the early years, to protect his medical practice, he published his work anonymously. But he became well known and was elected Fellow of the Royal Society at the early age of twenty-one. At twenty-eight, he was appointed a professor of physics at the Royal Institution. While he did resume work as a physician, his polyvalence brought to him varied assignments, such as assessing the dangers of using gas for street lighting in London, a state study of the precise length of a pendulum that had a swing period of two seconds, and superintendence of navigation and cartography.

In Young's own assessment, the most important of his

contributions to the sciences was his work on the nature of light. The understanding of light, until the seventeenth century, was only of the rudimentary, gross features. These were that light moved in straight lines, could throw a shadow and that a beam of light would bend when it passed through a slab of glass, ice or water. The lens, which focused a beam of light, was known and so was the spectrum. Of the nature of light, with its principal property of moving in straight lines, the simplest explanation (one espoused by Newton) was that light consisted of very small, weightless particles.

The particle theory, however, could not explain finer things, like the fringes that appear at the edges of images or the dappled look of light that comes through a cover of trees. In 1678, Huygens had developed an alternate theory, first proposed by Hooke, that light moved as waves. This theory was able to account for the known properties of light, but was in opposition to the strongly supported particle theory.

Young stepped in with a more analytical wave theory. Even during his early days as a medical student, Young had presented a thesis on the nature of sound waves. A few years later, in 1800, he read a paper before the Royal Society, where he treated light like ripples on the surface of a pond and explained the more complex features of light. This paper still did not convince many scientists. His next submission, in 1801, where he described his famous double-slit experiment, however, quite settled the matter.

We have noticed that when waves of water that are coming in at the seashore meet the waves flowing back, they either add together and grow larger, or cancel each other, depending on their stage of rise or fall at the time when they meet. Waves move in the form of crests and troughs. If two crests or two troughs come together, the wave grows large. But if the crest of one wave meets the trough of the other, the waves effectively cancel each other. The space where the waves meet would, thus, have parts where the waves are large and parts where the water is almost still.

Young considered that if two sets of waves of light were to meet in this way, on the surface of a screen, there should be dark and bright patches, or lines, where the waves add to or cancel each other. To arrange for such trains of waves to study, Young used a narrow beam of light through a pinhole, and the beam was split into two by placing a card in its path. In the modern version of the experiment, we use a beam of light that falls on an opaque sheet that has two narrow slits placed close together. The slits then become separate sources of light waves that go on to strike a screen.

If the beam is passed through a single slit, in place of a pair of slits, we can see that there would be a single line of light on the screen, bright in the centre and gently spread out, regardless of the nature of light being a wave or a train of particles. When there are two slits, if the beam were a stream of particles, it would be like two single slits and there would be a pair of images. But, if the light emerging from the two slits were waves, then the waves that reach the centre of the screen would arrive there at the same stage of undulation, no doubt, to create a bright line. At points off the centre, however, this would not be true. A little off-centre, on both sides, the waves would reach just out of step, and, like waves in the sea, they would cancel each other to give us a dark fringe. Again, a little further from the centre, the waves would be in step again, to add and create a bright line, although not as bright as the line in the centre. In this way, the pattern would be a series of fringes, alternately bright and dark (see Figure 16).

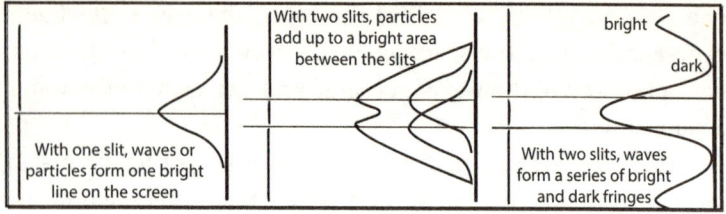

With two slits, particles add up to a bright area between the slits

bright

dark

With one slit, waves or particles form one bright line on the screen

With two slits, waves form a series of bright and dark fringes

Figure 16

Young could see that this would happen with the image as long as light was a wave, and he set up the experiment to test just that. What he found was a clear, unmistakable pattern, which would be unimaginable if light were to consist of particles, but is entirely reasonable when we consider light as a wave. While the fringes were only light and dark when the light used was of a single colour, with white light, the fringes split into the colours of the rainbow, as the positions where the waves add to or cancel each other are not the same for all the colours.

With this display, the wave theory of light got accepted and has never been challenged.

Young's achievements in science were as varied as his interests. In mechanics, he refined the existing ideas of the elastic behaviour of materials to define a single constant, known as 'Young's modulus', for a material, rather than different values for every bulk article. He explained the mechanism of the eye and the defects of vision when it focuses on objects at different distances. He was the first to suggest that colour vision arose from three kinds of nerve cells in the eye. In medicine, he studied the workings of the heart, and blood circulation. He was a scholar of languages and of the theory of comparative linguistics. He also made important contributions to the deciphering of Egyptian hieroglyphs. With his knowledge of sound waves, he carried out advanced studies into the theory of music and musical scales, with papers presented to the Royal Society.

With the European Renaissance well on its way, Young was a prime example of versatility.

Joseph-Louis Gay-Lussac

The findings of Boyle, Lavoisier and Dalton had given the world a glimpse of tiny constituents of matter—atoms—whose activity appeared before us as the properties of matter in bulk. The belief, however, was that it was a single atom of one element that combined with a single atom of another. Dalton, for instance, had considered water to consist of one atom each of hydrogen and oxygen—as HO—although we now know that the correct formula is H_2O.

This inner detail of how atoms combined came to us after more observation and contemplation, measurement and analysis of scraps of information and fitting the diverse information together, like pieces of a jigsaw puzzle. An early breakthrough came when French chemist Joseph-Louis Gay-Lussac took into account the volumes of gases, rather than their masses, when they combined. The pioneering work of Gay-Lussac set into motion a series of discoveries that refined the atomic theory and made it a powerful tool to understand matter.

Gay-Lussac was born in 1778 in Saint-Léonard-de-Noblat, northwestern France. He showed great talent from his early years and entered Ècole Polytechnique in Paris when he was nineteen. He worked with noted scientists and displayed outstanding skill in experimental work and, in time, was made the professor of chemistry at the Ècole.

Gay-Lussac had an abiding interest in gases. The experiments he carried out included daring studies at high altitudes by flying at a height of over 7,000 m in a gondola suspended from a lighter-than-air balloon. He collected samples of air at different altitudes and recorded changes in temperature and humidity as the balloon rose. However, as the altitude, although frighteningly high, was in the lower part of the atmosphere, he could detect no change in the composition of the air.

Gay-Lussac was appointed professor of physics at the Sorbonne, Paris; to the chair of chemistry at the Jardin des Plantes, the main botanical garden and an important research institute in France, and as a Foreign Member of the Royal Swedish Academy of Sciences. He was also elected to the Upper House of the French Parliament and was later appointed a Foreign Honorary Member at the American Academy of Arts and Sciences, Massachusetts, U.S.

Although Gay-Lussac was highly regarded, his major contribution in progressing science was one that he formulated early in his career, in 1808. His monograph describing the discovery, however, remained largely ignored and surfaced only in 1860, when an Italian chemist convinced the community of chemists in an international congress of its importance. This discovery was that when gases chemically combine, the ratio between the volumes of the reactant gases—and the product, if it is also gaseous—can be expressed in simple whole numbers.

For instance, when hydrogen and oxygen combine to produce water vapour, two volumes of hydrogen combine with one volume of oxygen—both volumes being measured at the same pressure and temperature—to produce two volumes of water vapour. This makes for a ratio of 2:1:2. So far, what had been noted was that masses of the gases and the vapour were in the ratio of 1:8:9. This was not a simple ratio, but it made sense, as $1 + 8 = 9$.

What Gay-Lussac found was that when volumes were considered, the volumes at the start did not add up to the volume at the end, but the volumes involved were in ratios of simple whole numbers. In the case of water, for instance, the ratio is 2:1:2, which is much simpler than 1:8:9, the ratios of the masses. That this was an observation of importance was not realized, as noted earlier, for many years. It was, however, the vital clue that led to understanding the units that participated in chemical reactions. Soon after Gay-Lussac's publication, Amedeo Avogadro came up with a stroke of insight that provided a theoretical basis for Gay-Lussac's observation. The two, together, made it possible for chemists of the future to work with substances in bulk as if they were dealing with the constituents themselves of the substances at the microscopic level.

Gay-Lussac is also known for his law, that the pressure of a gas that is kept at the same volume increases with the temperature when it is heated, a fact that he discovered while developing an air thermometer. The later part of his work, however, concentrated on chemistry. He studied processes and developed methods of quantitative analysis and laboratory equipment.

Amedeo Avogadro

It was through baby steps that it was understood that the elements, which constituted matter, consisted of basic, exceedingly minute particles called atoms. These participated in reactions with atoms of other elements, to form equally minute combinations of different atoms, of which all compounds were composed. Dalton had put out the idea in broad terms, and had even calculated the relative masses of what he considered to be the entities, which were the atoms. And Gay-Lussac, working with gases, made a significant observation that when gases participated in a reaction, the volumes of the different gases were always in the ratio of small whole numbers.

The field, however, was still wide open. Dalton had made a great advance, but the structure and nature of atomic entities taking part in chemical reaction had not been understood in a way that was of practical use. It was Amedeo Avogadro who considered the known information about chemical reactions and then the observation by Gay-Lussac, and deduced a sensitive detail of what must be going on down in that atomic world.

At first, he considered that the minute particles, of which a gas was made up, could be of different kinds—molecules, consisting of atoms, and 'elementary molecules', which would be what we now call 'single atoms'. He then concluded that equal volumes of gases (even different gases) contained the same numbers of the respective molecules. When the truth of these assertions was recognized, they brought about a revolution in the science of chemistry. Chemical reactions were recognized at the level of participating atoms, and the manner of participation could be probed and tested by experiment.

Avogadro was born in 1776 in Turin. His father was a leading lawyer and young Avogadro also trained to be a lawyer. Although he did well and had a career to look forward to, his interest lay in the sciences and he drifted away from the law and into scientific study and research. The original work that he did in the field of electricity was soon noticed and, at the age of thirty-three, he was appointed professor of physics at Royal College at Vercelli, northern Italy.

It was soon after Avogadro joined Vercelli, in 1811, that he published his celebrated paper, which built on the work of Dalton and Gay-Lussac, and reasoned that if whole numbers of volumes of different gases took part in reactions (and the reactions had to be of whole numbers of atoms, as atoms were indivisible), then the separate volumes must contain the same numbers of atoms. For instance, if two volumes of hydrogen combine with one volume of oxygen to produce two volumes of water, then, it is reasonable to suppose that two atoms of hydrogen combine with one atom of oxygen to produce two molecules of water, and each volume of the gases (and vapour) involved contain the same number of molecules.

We now know that the reaction is like this:

$$2H_2 + O_2 = 2H_2O$$

In the early nineteenth century, however, when physics and chemistry were in nascent stages, this formula was not on hand and the concept of the atom itself was undefined. The reality of atoms, in fact, was not wholly accepted till the beginning of the twentieth century, when studies on Brownian motion (named after the Scottish botanist, Robert Brown, who first researched the erratic movement of particles in a fluid) showed that tiny, but visible particles suspended in a gas, shift and move as a result of buffets from the molecules of the gas. It was in this condition, of no understanding of the nature of the atom, that Avogadro made the suggestion that has come to be known as Avogadro's hypothesis, and even as Avogadro's Law.

Still, the hypothesis remained ignored, while science floundered in some confusion for the next half century. It was in 1860 that Stanislao Cannizzaro, an Italian chemist who had discovered the worth of Avogadro's work, insisted before a science convention in Karlsruhe, Germany, that an answer to the current impasse in chemistry was before them! Yet, it took some years of relentless lobbying before the community realized that Gay-Lussac and Avogadro had unearthed a valuable secret of the nature of matter.

The effect of this on the fields of chemistry and physics was like never before. The quantitative study of chemical reactions became possible and brought about deep understanding and control of experiments for more discoveries and industrial processes. The behaviour of gases could be analysed with the laws of mechanics and the kinetic theory became meaningful and got firmly established.

Gay-Lussac had died in 1850 and Avogadro in 1856. The best the Royal Society could do was to award the Copley medal to Cannizzaro.

Sadi Carnot

Today, we understand that what drives a petrol engine or a steam turbine is the drop in the temperature of a hot gas or vapour while it expands. But heat engines were there even before this was known. There are records that steam power was used in ancient times and as a means to pump water in the seventeenth century. English inventor Thomas Newcomen had developed a piston-operated steam engine in 1712 and Scottish inventor James Watt had built a 10-hp steam engine in 1781. The principle, of how heat was converted into mechanical energy, however, had not been understood. The nature of heat was something of a mystery and the current belief was the caloric theory, which considered heat to be a kind of fluid. Better understanding—like heat lost by a cooling object should be equal to the heat gained by the surroundings, that energy could not be created or destroyed, or a way to relate mechanical work and heat—came only well into the nineteenth century.

We now have detailed principles about the way heat engines work. A remarkable insight is that the flow of heat from a high to a low temperature, which drives an engine, represents the transformation of an ordered system into a disordered one. This was largely thanks to work in the nineteenth century, the foundations for which were laid down through a remarkable exercise of analysis and reasoning by Sadi Carnot, a young military engineer in France.

Nicolas Léonard Sadi Carnot was born in 1796, in Paris, to a family distinguished in science and in public life. At sixteen, he joined École Polytechnique in Paris. This was a school meant for military engineers, but it had a fine tradition of scholarship and research. The school boasted of distinguished men of science on its staff and many of Carnot's colleagues went on to do important work in science.

Carnot did not take to service in the military. After some years, he negotiated a position where he was free to follow other pursuits and finally, he quit altogether. He had been influenced by a noted scientist friend and also attended lectures in physics and chemistry, and soon became engrossed in studying the mechanics of steam engines.

Steam engines had become important in industry and there was a great effort to increase their efficiency. There was a belief that great power was there in steam, and in the internal combustion engine, which had been recently invented. The efficiency of the steam engine, however, has been estimated to have been not more than 3 per cent.

Carnot's researches centred on two questions. The first was whether there were limits to the energy, theoretically, which could be obtained from a source of heat; and the second, whether other fluids or gases could replace steam in heat engines. He recorded his study of the two questions in his first and only book, *Reflections on the Motive Power of Fire*, in 1824, when he was just twenty-eight years of age. The book was a general survey and for the most part, was a descriptive account of the existing heat engines. It spoke of the different aspects of design and included some suggestions for improvements. In addition to these, however, the book contained a portion that abstracted the essential features of the general heat engine, which used not steam or air heated by gasoline, but just a 'working substance', and calculated the qualities of an 'ideal' engine.

This was one of the first attempts to strip the existing heat engines from the practical features that affected each one of them in their own way, and to find out the principles that governed all heat engines. Carnot's work laid down the bases for the theoretical investigation of heating and cooling in action— the field of thermodynamics. Exact calculations could then be made and answers to the question that he had asked could be attempted.

Carnot imagined all heat engines to be basically arrangements where a 'working substance' at a higher temperature performed work in the course of cooling to a lower temperature. It was then raised to the higher temperature by some source of energy, so that it could again perform work in the process of cooling. This was the cycle in which the engine continuously produced work, while consuming energy from the external source.

Carnot abstracted this process as a gas or a vapour that first gained heat when its container was placed on a 'source' at a higher temperature. In the process, the volume of the substance increased. Next, the container was placed on an insulator, so that it neither gained nor lost heat and was allowed to expand. This expansion, without any entry of heat, caused a drop in pressure and the gas also cooled to a lower temperature. The changes in pressure and volume can be seen in the lines A and B in the graph in Figure 17. During the second phase, 'B', however, no part of the heat gained in the first phase was lost.

The third step was that the container was placed on a 'sink', which was at the lower temperature and the sink absorbed heat, while the working substance was compressed. During compression, the heat gained in the first phase was lost to the 'sink'. The compression, accompanied with the loss of heat, caused a reduction of the volume and rise in the pressure. Finally, the container was again placed on the insulator and compressed. The volume reduced, the pressure increased and the temperature rose, so that the working substance was back to where it started.

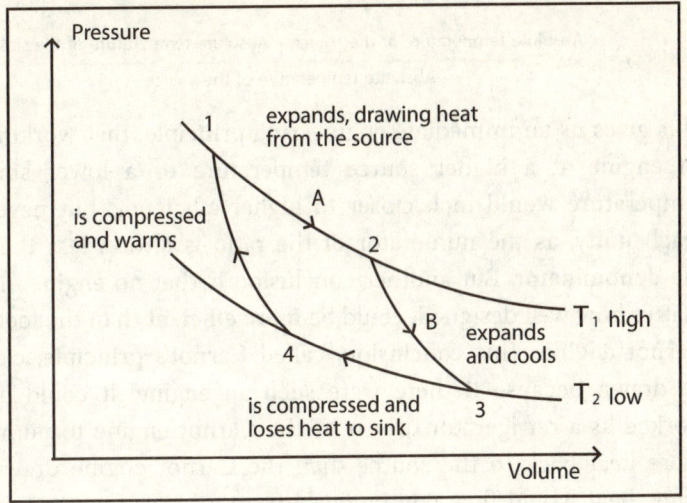

Figure 17

Carnot deduced that the work done by the substance, and the energy transferred from the 'source' to the 'sink' in the course of the cycle, were represented by the area of the curved oblong that the lines in the graph enclose.

An important feature of the process described is that in an ideal condition, it is reversible. In the reverse operation, work equal to the area enclosed by the lines would be done on the system and heat would be transported from the reservoir at the lower temperature, to the higher temperature—a reversal of the 'source' and the 'sink'. This is what happens in the case of a refrigerator.

Coming to the initial question that Carnot had posed—of how efficient a heat engine could become—we can now calculate the efficiency of his ideal engine. As the efficiency is the ratio of the work extracted to the energy drawn from the hot source, it can be worked out that:

$$\text{Efficiency} = \frac{\text{Absolute temperature of the source} - \text{Absolute temperature of the sink}}{\text{Absolute temperature of the source}}$$

This gives us an immediate engineering principle, that working an engine at a higher source temperature or a lower sink temperature would inch closer to higher efficiency, but never reach unity, as the numerator of the ratio is always less than the denominator. But another conclusion is that no engine, no matter how well designed, could be more efficient than the ideal Carnot engine. This conclusion, called Carnot's principle, can be drawn because if there were such an engine, it could be worked as a refrigerator driven by the Carnot engine to pump more heat back to the source than the Carnot engine draws. Thus, heat would flow continuously from a lower temperature to a higher temperature, which is the opposite of what we see.

After setting down these fundamentals of thermodynamics, Carnot left the military when he was thirty-two, and at thirty-six, he was taken ill with 'mania' and 'general delirium' and died soon after. But the work he did in this short life set the stage for a very comprehensive theory of the exchange of energy within systems—mechanical or chemical—that brought about the transformation of our relationship with nature during the following century.

Michael Faraday

Technologies that separate the modern world from the primitive or the medieval are surely electricity and magnetism. While the phenomena have long been known, their proper understanding took nearly a century. There were methods to create and store electric charges, but it was with the Voltaic Pile, in 1820, that the electric current could be studied. That an electric current deflected a magnetic needle was discovered by Ørsted in 1820, followed by the work of Ampère. In 1831, Michael Faraday discovered the reverse: that moving a magnetic field would induce a current in a conductor. Finally, there was the elegant unification of all these discoveries by James Clerk Maxwell in 1873.

The crucial step in the sequence, however, was the creation of electric current from magnetism, by Faraday.

Born a poor blacksmith's son, in 1791, near London, Faraday had to start working, doing odd jobs for a bookseller, even before he had much of an education. As a bright worker, he was soon taken as apprentice to a bookbinder. This occupation exposed him to books of all kinds, which made up for the formal education that he had missed. Two books—*Encyclopaedia Britannica* and Jane Marcet's *Conversations on Chemistry*—of which he made mention, years later, led him to develop a deep interest in the fields of electricity and chemistry.

Faraday also regularly attended lectures by the celebrated Sir Humphrey Davy, who had discovered many metals and elements using the method of electrolysis, and was a popular speaker. In time, on the strength of the notes that he had taken during the lectures, Faraday was accepted as an assistant to Davy at the latter's laboratory.

Faraday soon became adept at electrolysis and the experimental methods of the day. He also accompanied Davy on a tour of Europe and got to meet eminent men of science, including Volta, the inventor of the Voltaic Cell. The exposure planted in Faraday an abiding desire to go deeper into the nature and uses of electricity.

The state of knowledge at the time was mainly of the chemical effects of electricity, in which Faraday's master, Davy, had made a mark. It was discovered that electric currents could deflect a magnetic needle. The Voltaic Pile itself was a case of chemical effects giving rise to an electric current. As electric currents were found to give rise to magnetic effects, a question that Faraday asked was: can magnetic effects also give rise to electric currents?

A first discovery that Faraday made, in this quest, was that electric currents, as a source of magnetism, could give rise to mechanical forces. Ørsted and Ampère had shown that electric currents exercised a force on magnets. In Faraday's first experiment, a conductor was suspended with its lower end dipped, at a slant, into a dish of mercury, as shown in Figure 18. A bar magnet was fixed upright in the dish, so that one pole was just above the surface of mercury. Now, when a current was passed through the suspended rod, by way of the mercury, the rod was seen to move around the magnetic pole in a circle. The other way round—with a movable magnet and a fixed electric wire—had the same effect, as shown in the Figure.

We can readily see that the current in the conductor created a magnetic effect, which reacted with the force created by the bar magnet, and hence caused the conductor or the magnet to move. What had been discovered was nothing but the basic mechanism of the electric motor, which has led to the powerful motors at the heart of current day machinery, like railway locomotives, and the delicate motors in nano devices. Faraday, however, did not follow up this discovery, both as his interest was more in the principle rather than practical application or profit, and because there arose an unseemly controversy about the priority of the discovery, with none less than Davy.

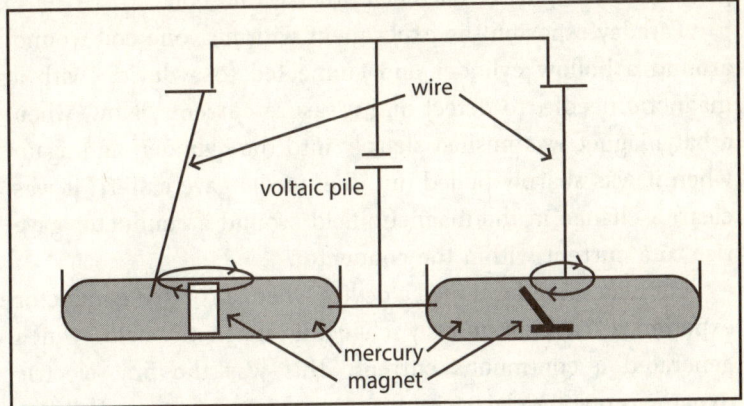

Figure 18

For some years, Faraday withdrew from research in electricity and devoted himself to electrolysis. Here, his meticulous measurements and records helped him discover the famous Faraday's Law: that the quantity of a substance liberated or produced during electrolysis is proportionate to the quantity of electric charge passed through the medium, and, secondly to the comparative weight of the atomic structure of the substance. This was itself a momentous discovery, which made electrolysis an exact and industrial process.

Some years later, he returned to his old question: of creating a current using magnetism. His apparatus this time was a coil of copper wire wound around a cylinder, with another coil, separated from the first by a layer of cloth. One coil was connected to a long wire that went past a magnetic needle. The other coil was connected to a Voltaic Pile. When the current was turned on, the magnetic needle was thrown to one side. When the current was turned off, the needle was thrown again. It seemed that turning the current on and off in the first coil gave rise to a spurt of current in the second coil!

Faraday repeated the experiment with just one coil wound around a hollow cylinder and connected to a device, with a magnetic needle, to detect and measure currents. Now, when a bar magnet was pushed sharply into the cylinder, and again when it was sharply pulled out, the needle gave a start. It was clear: a change in the magnetic field around a conductor gave rise to a current within the conductor.

Faraday soon developed a device where a rotated conductor experienced a continuously changing magnetic field, which generated a continuous current. This was the first electric dynamo, creating electricity from mechanical energy. The idea has now been developed to sophistication, generating electricity from steam turbines, flowing water and the wind. It is also used in a simple speedometer, which measures how fast a wheel is moving from the current that a connected dynamo produces.

Here again, Faraday left the development of his discovery to others and turned his attention to the principle. He combined the work of Ampère (of magnetism from electricity) with his own (of electricity from a changing magnetic field), and laid the foundations for later work, where the knowledge about electric charges and magnetism was integrated. This led to the understanding of electromagnetic waves (of which even light is an instance) and the many wonders of the modern world.

Charles Darwin

Darwin's theory of evolution is a scientific discovery that changed the concept of humans as a special part of creation and placed all living things within the same biological process. Just as the discoveries of Copernicus brought to the common mind the scientific understanding of the wonders of the night sky, Charles Darwin brought rationality and science into understanding the variety of plants and animals, and traced a path that connects the history of all of them.

Darwin was born in 1809, in a well-to-do family in Shrewsbury, England. At the time, there was little other than the Biblical theory of creation to explain living things that inhabited the earth. It was the mind of Darwin, curious to a fault and passionately interested in nature, aided by the extensive and systematic study of an exotic array of living things, that helped unravel the secret of natural selection—the mechanism that drove species to undergo changes in the course of adapting to changing physical conditions.

Even as a young boy, Darwin was fascinated by insects and the world of living things. His father, a leading doctor, wished his son to follow the same profession. Darwin, hence, joined the University of Edinburgh to study medicine. But Darwin had other interests, including contemplation about the origins of life, and the plans for him to be a doctor were soon given up. He then joined the University of Cambridge to study for a profession in the clergy at least. Darwin did go through the course of study with reasonable success, but he spent most of his time studying geology and with a group of botanists and zoologists on expeditions to different parts of England in search of rock, plant, insect and animal specimens.

He qualified, at the age of twenty-two, but was spared a life as a minister of the church when he was offered a position as a naturalist to accompany a two-year voyage to the South American coastline. His father was aghast, but was finally persuaded to fund his participation, and Darwin set sail on an adventure that lasted five years.

Biologists, even more than others, were aware of the great diversity of plant and animal forms there was in the world. But how such great variety could have come to be was an equally great, unanswered question. Even the position that all living things were created by God was challenged to explain why the Creator should have given rise to countless categories. A leading theory, put forward by the naturalist Jean-Baptiste Lamarck, was that of the transmutation of species. This theory did not consider that living things had a common ancestor, but that the simplest creatures arose continuously through spontaneous generation. These creatures were infused with a life force that drove them to progressively greater complexity. The theory was clearly not up to explaining the many questions that arose, and Darwin, who had been associated as a student with Robert Grant, an anatomist who subscribed to the theory, was as puzzled as he had been when he started.

The voyage to South America turned out to be an exposure, all at once, to an extent of diversity of species that was clearly not feasible in ordinary field expeditions and visits to botanical or zoological gardens. The voyage down the eastern coast, with excursions inland, exposed Darwin to nobles, savages, tribals, bandits, serpents, turtles, animals, fossils, dangers and wonders. An observer, reporter and collector as he was, he curated samples and specimens, and descriptions and records, and sent them back to England from every port of call.

After sailing around the coast of South America, the expedition ship, called the Beagle, berthed at Galápagos Islands, an equatorial, volcanic archipelago to the west of South America. Here, in an ancient region unspoilt by civilization, Darwin saw specimens of great antiquity, and birds, fish, animals and insects of great variety but still basic similarity. Turtles in one island, for instance, were just a little different from those in another, so much so that one person boasted that he could identify an island by what turtles were found there. There were birds of the same species in the islands but they had different kinds of beaks. Were these instances of adaptation to different conditions? A suspicion began to grow in Darwin's mind that maybe these different types had descended from a common ancestor. And if this could be within a species, why not with different species? And if this had happened, how was it brought about?

At the end of five years, in 1836, when Darwin returned, he was already a celebrity because of the material that he had sent back. His account of the expedition, *A Naturalist's Voyage around the World*, was published with great success and he was elected to prestigious bodies.

Darwin settled with his wife in Kent, in the south of England and spent the next twenty years in contemplation, and in studying the vast data he had gathered. He knew that domestic animals were bred to promote selected qualities, but this was done by controlling the course of nature. How could it take place in the wild?

It was the writings of the economist, Thomas Robert Malthus, which gave Darwin a lead to find the answer. Malthus had written that the growth of population was geometric, which was faster than the rise of resources. This would cause shortages and humans would have to compete for survival. Darwin noted that this was the case with animals, which were always at the number that the environment could support. Their survival was, hence, competitive and only the fittest could survive.

Yes, this was the answer—the survival of the fittest. This was the engine that selected those individuals in a species that had the features best fitted to thrive in changing conditions. It was nature's hand imposing the breeder's rules. It was the mechanism that explained how thousands of species had arisen around the world, over the millions of years of its history. It enabled tracing a continuous line from the ancient, single-celled organism to lizards, fish, mammals, apes and humans.

Darwin set forth his theory in 1859 in *The Origin of the Species*, a work that examines the geography and geology of the places where different species are found and traces the conditions that influenced their features. The Theory of Evolution was a sensation that electrified the scientific community. Gregor Mendel soon published the bases of heredity, which fleshed out the mechanism of evolution and a grand scheme was found to underlie the wonder of the natural world.

Opposition to the theory was plentiful and continues to this day. But the mass of data that has collected after the direction that the theory gave to anthropologists has put the Theory of Evolution beyond question and made it part of common awareness.

Gregor Mendel

Genetic engineering—the manipulation of the DNA of living things—has become an industry of vast economic and social significance. We are now able to identify genetic markers of disease and sometimes carry out a correction. We can modify the genome of plants for better productivity or stability. We can even use genetic methods to assemble drugs and synthesize materials.

The beginning of it all was the 1865 paper submitted by Gregor Mendel, an Augustinian friar and abbot of St Thomas's Abbey, in Brno, now in the Czech Republic. Till that time, the existence of heredity was generally known, in terms of the similarity of children born to the same parents and practices followed while breeding animals, but there was no scientific study or inkling of how heredity came about.

Mendel was born in 1822 in a small, Austrian village, to a German-speaking family. It was a poor, farming family and Mendel worked as a gardener and beekeeper during his early school years. His sister parted with her inheritance to help him through the Palacký University Olomouc, where he studied philosophy and physics and was exposed to the research of hereditary traits of plants and animals. At the recommendation of his teachers, he moved to the Augustine monastery at Altbrünn, known as a centre of learning, so that he could continue his studies.

When he was ordained as a priest, however, he found he was ill-suited to work as a minister and his duties were changed to teaching. Here again, he could not pass qualifying trials, but was engaged as an assistant teacher for several years. Despite not qualifying, he was quite successful because of his enquiring mind and persistence, and his gentle and kindly ways. He was also free to indulge his sense of wonder about the hidden mystery of life. With a background of farming and exposure to science, he was aware of the variety of colour, size and form of animals and plants of the same species and wished to understand how it came about.

It was during these years in the monastery that he carried out, in the garden in the monastery grounds, his eight-year-long studies of the generations of the pea plant. He concentrated on this plant as its successive generation could be easily and rapidly created in a nursery and its varieties had simple differentiating features.

Some of these simple features were the height of the plants, the shape of the pods, and the texture and colour of the seeds. These were contrasting features—for example, plants were tall or they were short, pods were loose or tight, seeds were yellow or green—and Mendel wished to discover how the traits were passed on from parent to offspring.

A feature of the pea plant is that the flower has both its reproductive organs: the anthers with pollen; and the stigma, securely enclosed in the petals. It is hence difficult for the pollen of one flower to travel to another flower and then to reach the stigma. The most likely form of reproduction is, hence, self-pollination. This is the reason that the offspring of pure strains usually had the same features. As Mendel wished to experiment with different strains, he cut open the early bud, removed the stamen and then deposited pollen from another plant, of a different pure strain, on the stigma.

During this cross-fertilization, Mendel selected strains with contrary features: for example, a pure, tall strain with a pure, short (or dwarf) strain. This provided him with a stock of first-generation hybrids. Then, he cross-fertilized the hybrids with each other and with pure strains. With the resulting second-generation hybrids, he again carried out cross-fertilization trials, and kept careful records of the sequences of cross-fertilization and the features of the resulting mixed strains.

The results he obtained were consistently that when pure strains with contrary forms of a feature were cross-bred, all offspring had the feature of one of the parents. He called this feature 'the dominant feature' and the other feature 'the recessive feature'. But when the hybrids were cross-fertilized with one another, three-fourths (on the average) of the resulting second generation had the dominant feature, but a fourth had the recessive feature.

Further cross-fertilization trials revealed that of the three with the dominant feature, one (on the average) was a pure strain with the dominant feature while the other two were hybrids. The one with the recessive feature was a pure strain with the recessive feature.

Mendel collected these simply stated results over eight painstaking years of well-documented experiment and verification. Finally, he was able to write down the rules that appeared to be followed in inheritance. He named the reason for the appearance of a feature 'a factor' that corresponded to the feature. He reasoned that the factors occurred in pairs and a pure strain had a pair of the factor for a trait. When a pair of individuals with contrary factors was cross-bred, the offspring inherited one factor from each parent and ended up with one factor of each of the two kinds. As one of the factors was dominant, the offspring displayed the dominant feature. Now, when these offspring were cross-bred, the second-generation offspring could receive three combinations of factors. The first, which would occur one-fourth of the times, was of both dominant factors. The second, which would occur half the times, was one factor of both kinds. And the third, which would again occur one-fourth of the times, was both recessive factors.

The second-generation offspring with both dominant factors would be a pure, dominant strain; the ones with both factors would be hybrids, like their parents, while the ones with both recessive factors would be a pure, recessive strain.

This more or less, sums up the knowledge of genetics that we have today. In this age, we understand the nature of the 'factors', which we call genes. We know their molecular nature and have developed methods to snip and splice the millions-of-units-long DNA molecule. But the start was the patient and systematic research by an obscure priest in a rural monastery, who had the clear-sightedness to seek out one of nature's most powerful secrets.

Louis Pasteur

That the tissue of living things had a structure was unknown to the generations before the seventeenth century, when the microscope was invented. And only later in that century was the invisible world of microorganisms discovered by Leeuwenhoek. But it took until the nineteenth century, and the Frenchman Louis Pasteur, for the role that microbes played in health and disease to be understood.

Pasteur was born in 1822 in the mountainous Jura region of France. He showed no great promise in his early years and the talent that he showed was in art. But he persevered with science and received his master's from École normale supérieure in Paris. After some years at the universities of Strasbourg and Lille, he returned to Paris in 1857 as the director of scientific studies at the École. Ten years later, he became the chair of organic chemistry at the Sorbonne University. Finally, in 1887, he established the Pasteur Institute of which he became the director.

His early work was with the structure of crystals. The structure of some crystals, like quartz, and of the molecules in some solutions, even sugar solution, is such that they affect light when it passes through them. Light consists of electric and magnetic waves, whose undulations are in a plane perpendicular to the direction of the waves. This is like the waves on the surface of water, where the motion of water is up and down, while the wave moves over the horizontal surface. In the case of light waves, however, there is no limitation of 'up and down' and the vibration can be in any direction: up-down, left-right or at a slant. When the vibration is restricted to one plane, it is said that the light has been polarized. Now, some crystals and some solutions rotate the plane of polarization of light that passes through them, by an angle.

The study of crystals had revealed that there were substances that existed in two forms, each chemically the same as the other, but differing in their effect on polarized light. Tartaric acid was one of these. Pasteur, in his researches, noted that the two kinds of crystals themselves had different structures, one being the mirror image of the other. It is believed that it was Pasteur's training as an artist that enabled him to make this out. The discovery soon led to the understanding that such features of asymmetric crystals arose from asymmetry in the structure of the molecules, and this led to advances in the science of chemistry and crystallography.

The field in which Pasteur is best known, however, is that of fermentation and the process of pasteurization, by which food is treated to stay free from decay for long periods. The fermentation of sugars in malt and grape juice, by yeast, to form beer and wine respectively, is a major industry. A great concern in this trade was that the beer or wine often spoiled, and Pasteur had been commissioned to find a solution. In the course of his study, Pasteur found that the spoilage occurred because of a competing process caused by bacteria, to ferment the sugar into acetic acid (one of the components of vinegar), instead of into alcohol.

Pasteur also discovered that maintaining beer or wine at a high temperature for a few hours killed the offending organisms and prevented spoilage. This process, named pasteurization, is the way that milk and many other food products are now treated to have greater shelf life.

While pasteurization has its uses, the truly important thing that Pasteur had discovered was that microorganisms could bring about chemical changes. Until that time, the causes of natural processes and diseases were believed to be living things that arose spontaneously from organic matter. The germ theory had been proposed, but it was Galen's theory of 'miasmas' that held sway with physicians. Pasteur, by his celebrated 'swan neck flask' experiment, showed conclusively that organisms were not 'generated' but had to enter from the exterior.

The apparatus for this experiment was a flask that contained nutrient-rich material, connected to the exterior through an S-shaped neck, as shown in Figure 19. When the mixture was boiled, all organisms in it were killed or deposited at the further reaches of the tube. The flask could then be allowed to remain open for weeks, with no decay or growth of microorganisms. It was only if the flask were tilted and dust or other things trapped in the neck were allowed to enter, that the growth started.

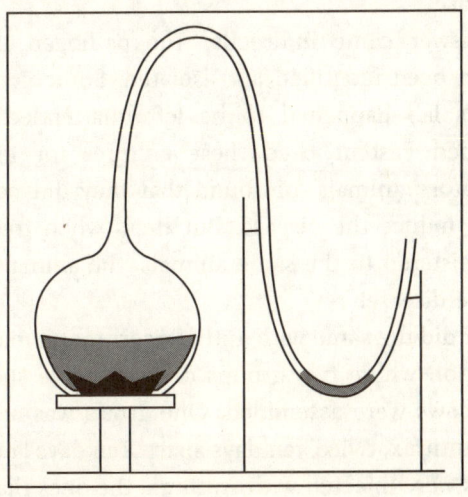

Figure 19

This was a dramatic demonstration that the entry of microbes from the exterior was necessary and it showed that hygiene in the manufacture of beer and wine was the way to save the process from spoilage. But more importantly, it established that diseases were caused by microorganisms. While the link between hygiene and health was understood, this was also the start of the science of microbiology.

Pasteur's other great achievement was the discovery of vaccines. Anthrax was a deadly disease that affected cattle. The pathogen that caused the disease had been identified, but there seemed to be no way to prevent it. Pasteur, who was called in by the ministry of agriculture, had noticed that at a place where cattle, which had died of anthrax, had been buried, earthworms bought up the soil from below to the surface. Samples of this earth, when injected in guinea pigs, caused the disease. Pasteur's solution, that farmers should burn and not bury the dead anthrax-affected animals, put an end to the crisis, but not to the disease.

The answer came indirectly. The pathogen that caused cholera had been identified and isolated. Some germ cultures in Pasteur's lab happened to be left unattended for a few weeks. When Pasteur used these cultures for his research with laboratory animals, he found that they did not have the capacity to induce the disease. But then, when fresh cultures were administered to the same animals, the animals were able to resist the disease!

Pasteur did the same with anthrax germs and made a public demonstration where two groups of twenty-five sheep, a goat and some cows were assembled. One group was administered weakened anthrax, twice, ten days apart. Ten days later, when all the animals were injected with Anthrax, the ones that had been protected stayed healthy while the rest perished within a day!

Pasteur is also immortal for his discovery of the Rabies vaccine. He had identified the rabies pathogen and found, in his research, that an animal that had been affected could resist the progress of the disease if administered a weakened strain several times over two weeks. An occasion arose when a child was bitten by a rabid dog and would, by all reckoning, succumb to rabies. Pasteur dared to inject the child with the rabies pathogen that had been weakened by exposure to air. When the child recovered, it was clear that treatment for a horrible scourge had been found!

Joseph Lister

It would be difficult for us in the modern world to imagine unclean operating theatres, but during much of the nineteenth century, even surgeons did not concern themselves with cleanliness. There is a celebrated illustration of 1846, which shows the first time an operation being carried out with ether as an anaesthetic. It shows a surgeon and his assistants in their town clothes; even the patient has his shoes on. In fact, in those days, it was quite common even for a tradesman or a passing dog to enter and leave such 'operation theatres' as they pleased.

In those days, as anaesthesia was not used, a patient would often be drugged with rum and then held firmly by well-built surgical assistants. The hallmark of a great surgeon was that he could do the operation quickly, both to shorten the agony as well as to expose the wound for as short a time as possible. It was rare if surgery was not followed by serious infection, septicaemia or gangrene, and led to actual recovery.

All this changed with the work of Joseph Lister, the English surgeon, who discovered antiseptics. The use of antiseptics in surgery and in infirmaries marked not just a dramatic reduction in fatalities but also the awareness in the medical profession that it was a battle between a patient's body and hordes of microscopic pathogens that a physician was managing.

Lister was born in 1827 in London, the son of a prosperous businessman who was also an amateur scientist of some note. Lister trained to become a surgeon and attended University College in London, where he worked with the leading men of the day. They were all masters of anatomy, skilful in their trade and remarkable in their resourcefulness. It is said that surgeons would use a scalpel to scrape the table where the patient lay, and use the splinter to plug an artery.

The germ theory was yet to be accepted and the understanding was that the putrefying of a wound was because of poisons and microbes that were generated from within the wound. Hospitals were rank with the smell of death, and surgery, howsoever successful, was usually followed by infection and fatal complications.

While working as professor of surgery at the University of Glasgow, Lister came across the work of Pasteur, who found that food spoilage was because of the presence of living organisms. Lister carried out his own experiments and reasoned that this may be the reason for the decay of human tissue that was exposed in surgery. Pasteur's method to kill microorganisms was to warm liquids. This was clearly not possible with a surgical patient, but another of Pasteur's suggestions was a chemical wash, and this seemed to be practicable.

A recently discovered material, which was derived from coal tar and related to substances used to treat wood, was carbolic acid. After some experimenting, Lister decided to use this material to disinfect the instruments used in surgery. The first few surgeries performed with instruments and dressing that had been sprayed with carbolic acid took Lister by surprise. Till that time, the real engagement of the surgeon was after he had performed the first surgery, as he was always required to follow it up with more than one incision of gangrenous tissue or the amputation of a limb. But in the surgeries performed with the use of carbolic acid, there was almost no instance of infection!

Lister devised different ways of using disinfected dressing and plasters and showed that avoiding infection in the first place and then keeping the surroundings clean did wonders to improve surgical statistics. By just washing surgical instruments, it is said that the fatalities in his operations dropped from 45 per cent to 15 per cent. In a case of compound fracture, the use of lint soaked in carbolic acid was so impressive that Lister described the case through six articles in *Lancet*, the leading medical journal in 1867.

Lister became a popular medical lecturer and spread the message of antiseptics and asepsis in surgery. He set up the practice of surgeons scrubbing before operations and spraying the patient and the surroundings with carbolic acid. Surgery and the practice of medicine were transformed from a primitive procedure to a scientific activity.

It is not that there was no opposition. There were leading surgeons who thought Lister's ideas were worthless and even *Lancet* warned medical professionals against dangerous, 'progressive' ideas. But Lister's own papers in the same journal were so emphatic, and the results so evident, that using antiseptics was soon the norm and part of standard textbooks on surgical practice.

Lister was called upon to treat Queen Victoria herself for an abscess, where he used carbolic acid and used a rubber tube to drain the fluid while the wound healed. Carbolic acid was used in the battlefields during the Franco-Prussian war of 1871 and the results were impressive in the lives that were saved, which were sure to have been lost in the usual course.

Lister's discoveries are now the norm in medical practice. While operation theatres are temples of aseptic cleanliness, even the draft of air that blows over the patient is arranged in a way that it carries away a microbe that may happen to enter. Instruments are sterilized, and never used again. Incidental infection has become a rarity.

James Clerk Maxwell

The science of physics can be described as the representation, with measurement and numbers, of the way that physical things interact. The principle of the lever, the relationship between volume and mass, the geometric representation of planetary motion, the laws regarding gases, the laws of motion—they all express physical things with numbers. The same was done with the interaction of electricity and magnetism, with mathematical expressions of elegance and simplicity, and with a prediction of a thing as yet unseen. The prediction was soon found to be true, which validated the theory. This theory set the stage for bringing together different physical phenomena under a single principle, and in this respect, it placed physics apart from other sciences.

This description of all of electricity and magnetism with just four mathematical equations was the startling achievement of James Clerk Maxwell, in 1873, lately professor of natural philosophy at King's College, London.

Maxwell was born in 1831 in Edinburgh, Scotland, the only son of a lawyer-turned-landowner who invested quality time in nurturing the young man's undoubted talents. Even from the age of three, the young Maxwell showed persistent scientific curiosity and the desire to understand the working of mechanical things as well as all kinds of plants and animals. His father encouraged him by taking him on walks in the woods and to scientific talks and presentations. Even as a child, Maxwell could clearly grasp all that he saw and heard, and when he was just fourteen, he had devised a method to draw a perfect ellipse (an oval) using two pins and a piece of string. The method was presented to the Royal Society of Edinburgh, but by a distinguished professor on behalf of Maxwell, as the Society did not wish to be addressed by a lad so young!

After his school years, which were marked by original work in mathematics and optics to name a few achievements, Maxwell entered Cambridge, at eighteen. He continued at Trinity College, where he carried out studies on the mechanism of how we perceive colour and colour blindness, and was awarded the Royal Society's Rumford Medal. He also followed his early fascination with electromagnetism and studied Faraday's work. His paper, 'On Faraday's Lines of Force', which he read before the Cambridge Philosophical Society in 1855, drew admiration from Faraday himself, for the manner in which his work had been cast in mathematics!

For a while, he worked on a problem regarding the nature of Saturn's rings, which had been set as a contest for contemporary scientists. This involved deep mathematical analyses and the nature and behaviour of gases in orbit around a distant planet. Maxwell's entry, a sixty-eight page submission with more than 200 equations, was the winner. The analyses attracted the attention of scientists who were working with the kinetic theory of gases and this established Maxwell as a formidable mathematical physicist.

Before long, he came back to his interest in electricity and magnetism. Many of the properties of electric charges and electric currents were known. It had been shown that electric currents generated a magnetic field and also that a changing magnetic field would result in an electric current. The prospect of finding a relationship between electricity and magnetism was tantalizing. Maxwell, during his years as a professor at Trinity

College and then, at his country home in Scotland, applied his keen, mathematical mind to the problem.

Bit by bit, the mathematics took shape. One of the first facts about electric charges was that their effect reduced by the square of the distance. From this, Maxwell derived his first relation, of the total lines of force that passed through a closed surface, of any shape, which contained a quantity of charge. The next was about magnetism. Unlike charges that can be positive or negative, magnetic poles must come in pairs—for every north pole, there must be a south pole. Any closed surface would, thus, have as many lines of force going out as coming in. The second relation was, hence, a way of saying that the total lines of force would be zero. The next two relations describe the electric field that is produced when a magnetic field changes and the magnetic effects of an electric current.

These four relations, which were stated in 1873 in a form that has not been changed since then, express all that there is to know about electromagnetism. Another effect, which had not been observed but is implied by the Maxwell equations, is that when an electric charge oscillates, it will radiate energy in electric and magnetic waves. We can see that when a charge oscillates, it will induce an oscillating magnetic field too. The oscillating magnetic field, in turn, will induce an oscillating electric field, and so on, and the effects would spread out. The Maxwell equations, which were derived based only on what had been observed, quite naturally led to the generation of electromagnetic waves. When these very waves were detected in the 1890s, by Jagdish Chandra Bose and Guglielmo Marconi, it showed that Maxwell's equations had captured a fundamental feature of electricity and magnetism.

Maxwell had himself worked out the speed with which electromagnetic waves travel. He found that the speed was almost exactly the same as the best estimate then available of the speed of light. This was not surprising as light is also an electromagnetic wave, but one that is oscillating much more rapidly than radio waves. Maxwell's equations, it was found, could work out all the properties, like the refractive index or interference effects, of visible light.

Thanks to the deep insight encapsulated in the exact equations of Maxwell, the following decades had a tool to examine puzzling features of nature that were discovered. One was how frequencies of the radiation from a warm object were distributed. Then, the applications of electromagnetic waves—their transmission, wireless, microwave, and the interaction of light with atomic particles—followed. It was the apparently simple but powerful Maxwell equations that enabled the sophistication of technology through the twentieth century, inconceivable without the aid of the theory.

Wilhelm Conrad Röntgen

In algebra, a quantity whose value we do not know is identified by a symbol, usually denoted by the letter 'x'. A mysterious, invisible ray that was discovered in the lab in 1895 was named 'X-ray' for the same reason.

X-rays are a form of light that can pass through many materials that are normally opaque, and they are now in common use in hospitals and in industry. X-rays have always been there around us, but it was in the course of research into a frontier area of the passage of electricity through gases that Wilhelm Conrad Röntgen discovered this radiation and subsequently its properties.

Röntgen was born in Germany in 1845, but three years later, his father migrated to Holland. His early years can be described as academic disaster: he set out by being expelled from Utrecht Technical School for indiscipline. As he showed promise nevertheless, his father arranged for an admission to the University of Utrecht, but this was frustrated when the examiner turned out to have been at the earlier institution. Still, he was allowed to attend some of the programmes and finally joined the Polytechnic School in Zurich. Engineering, however, was not the subject of his liking and it was fortunate that he met an inspiring teacher of physics, whom he joined as an assistant.

In this role, Röntgen began to apply himself as he had never done before and rapidly came up-to-date with the principles and the current state of research in physics. He soon moved, with his mentor, to the University of Strasbourg, where he blossomed into a brilliant experimentalist with great technical skill in devising and building instruments and apparatus. On the strength of his work, he was soon elevated as a professor of physics at the Hessian University at Giessen, in Germany.

A subject of interest at the time was the passage of electricity through gases. It had been found that if metal plates connected to a powerful battery were placed some distance apart within a glass bulb from which the air had been partially evacuated, a current flowed and rays were projected between the plates. As the rays flowed from the negatively charged plate, they were called cathode rays, and the glass bulb was called a cathode ray tube. English physicist Sir William Crookes had found that the rays that moved in straight lines were affected by magnetic fields and produced a glow when they struck the sides of the glass bulb. The German, Philipp Lenard, created an aluminium window in the glass tube so that the rays could be passed out. But he found that they were absorbed by the air when they emerged. Lenard then had to pass them into a fully evacuated glass tube for the rays to be studied.

It was in this context that Röntgen, while working with a Lenard tube in his laboratory, noticed a curious phenomenon. Whenever he switched on the cathode ray tube, there was a flickering in one part of his working table. When he looked carefully, he saw that there was a card coated with barium platinocyanide, which had been left on the table. Whenever the cathode ray tube was switched on, the chemical on the card absorbed some invisible ray and emitted light.

Röntgen repeated the trial with different tubes and with the glass covered with cardboard so that it was light-tight and it was not the glow of the tube that was seen. The effect on the barium platinocyanide card was undoubtedly some rays that came from the cathode ray tube. He continued the trials to find the properties of the rays, including the materials that it could not pass through. He saw, for instance, that a sheet of lead would stop the rays from affecting the chemical-coated card screen. It was in the course of such a trial that he put his hand between the tube and the card, and saw on the screen, the outline of the bones of his hand! It was clear that the rays passed through the fleshy part of the hand but were stopped by the bones, and hence threw a shadow!

Röntgen was quick to report the discovery. He had first noticed the glow on the card on 8 November 1895, and his paper, *On a New Kind of Rays*, was published on 28 December 1895. Röntgen continued his research and published two more papers in the next two years. He established that the rays—'X-rays', as they were (and are) called—were generated when cathode rays impinged on a metal, and could be made more penetrating if the voltage applied to the cathode ray tube were increased.

An immediate application was to use the rays to throw shadows of bones, or even of dense tissue, onto a photographic plate, for use in medical diagnosis. Further applications are legion, in industry, for what is called 'non-destructive testing', just like a medical X-ray is a 'non-invasive' investigation. Soft X-rays are routinely used in metal detectors at airports. Hard X-rays affect human tissue and are used in the treatment of cancer. X-rays were also identified as light waves with a wavelength comparable to inter-atomic distances and have wide application in investigating crystal structure and in metallurgy.

Apart from its utility, however, the discovery of X-rays was among the perplexing features of the natural world that confronted scientists towards the end of the nineteenth century. The discovery set in motion a flurry of research into what made X-rays arise and led to an understanding of the structure of the atoms themselves—the stuff of physics in the twentieth century.

Joseph John Thomson

It was a watershed moment in the history of science when it became clear that the atom was not the ultimate unit of matter, but the different atoms themselves were composed of particles, perhaps combinations of the same particles. This clarity about the nature of the deep internals of an invisible world came through the outstanding experimental work of the Englishman, Joseph John Thomson, and the results that he announced to the scientific community in 1897.

Thomson was born in 1856 near Manchester, in England, to a family with a tradition of dealing with rare books, but little of science. As an avid reader and good student, a career in engineering was planned for him. He did well, and went on to Cambridge, where he took the mathematical tripos with distinction. He started work in theoretical physics and produced a major paper at the age of twenty-four. However, he did appreciate the need for skills in experimental work and settled down to work in Cavendish Laboratory, the physics department of Cambridge University.

In 1884, when Thomson was just twenty-eight years of age, Baron Rayleigh, the head of the laboratory, retired and he named Thomson as his successor. It was a controversial choice, as there were eminent men of greater experience. But Thomson was a successful leader of the laboratory for thirty-four years and he not only did outstanding work that got him the Nobel Prize for physics in 1906, but as many as eight of his students followed suit!

At the time, there was extensive knowledge about electricity and magnetism but only tentative ideas about how the properties of materials depended on atoms. A topic that seemed to connect the two was the passage of electricity through gases. It had been found that if high voltage was applied to a pair of metal plates in a glass tube from which air (or a gas) had been largely evacuated, a current passed and there was a glow of light in the tube. As the flow was from the negative plate, the stream was called 'cathode rays'. If there was a gap in the positive plate for the cathode rays to pass through and strike the glass, the glass began to glow. Cathode rays were also seen to be affected by a magnetic field, in the manner of an electric current flowing in the opposite direction.

William Crookes, who developed the Crookes tube, with the help of which cathode rays were discovered, had suggested that the rays consisted of negatively charged particles. A dominant theory, however, was that the rays were a form of radiation, like electromagnetic waves. This was strengthened by the fact that cathode rays were able to pass through a thin sheet of gold placed in their path.

A major objection to the idea that the rays were negatively charged particles was that, while the beam could be deflected by a magnetic field, an electric field did not affect the beam. The arrangement for deflecting the beam is shown in Figure 20. Thomson also tried it out with electric charges and with the same result. As the stream in the tube was clearly a current of charges, propelled by an electric potential and reacting to magnetic fields, he could not accept the fact that electric fields had no effect.

Thomson analysed what may be taking place and he reasoned that the stream of charged particles may have the effect of charging atoms of the gas. These charged atoms would then rush to the charged plates and neutralize them. Another mechanism may be that the charged plates induce the opposite charge on atoms of the gas, which collect around the plates and shield them. In either case, when there is some gas in the tube, the effect of electric charge gets weakened.

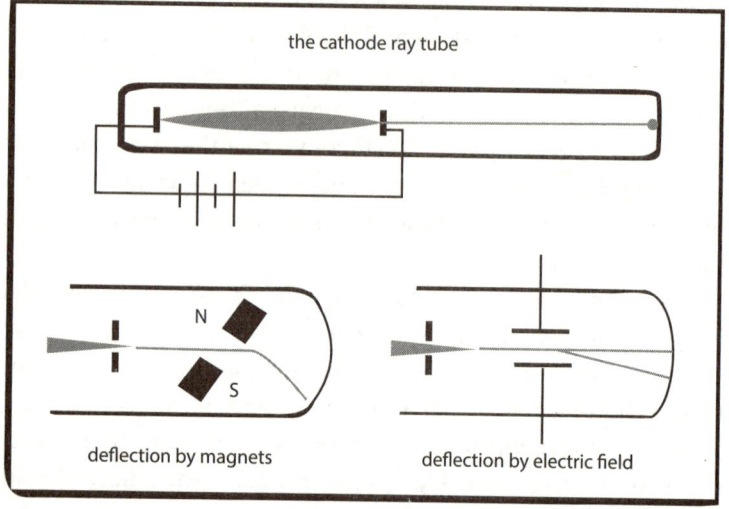

the cathode ray tube

deflection by magnets

deflection by electric field

Figure 20

Thomson now built a cathode ray tube where the air had been not partially, but thoroughly evacuated. This time, sure enough, the electric field deflected the cathode ray beam! This was success—Thomson had proved that the stream in the tube consisted of negatively charged particles. But where could the particles have come from but the atoms in the cathode?

What now remained was to determine some of the properties of the particles.

As the strength of the magnetic field and the electric field being applied was known, the extent of deflection of the beam indicated the speed of the particles and an estimate of the charge on the particles and their mass. The charge and mass could not be worked out independently, as the extent of the deflection depended on both the charge and the mass. The more the charge, the greater the deflection; the more the mass, the lesser the deflection. What could be worked out was the ratio of the charge to the mass, called the e/m ratio.

The speed of the cathode rays turned out to be more than 2,50,000 km/second. This is an extremely high speed, as that of light is just 3,00,000 km/second. The speed suggests a very light particle. As for the e/m ratio, this could be compared with the same ratio that was known for a stream of charged hydrogen atoms, and was found to be thousand times greater. If the charge was taken to be the same, the particles would need to be thousand times lighter than the hydrogen atom.

Thomson then worked on the cathode rays that were produced from the hot filament of an incandescent bulb and by cathodes made of different metals. He found that the e/m ratio was the same in all cases. This indicated that the particles in all the kinds of cathode rays were the same.

Thomson now announced the inescapable conclusion. First, that atoms had constituent parts, which could be separated by heat or electrical forces. And then, that the negatively charged particles that came from all atoms were the same and were lightweight: less than 1000th of the mass of the hydrogen atom. This was an electrifying announcement that spurred the scientific world and set in motion major programmes of continued research.

Thomson developed a theory of the structure of the atom as a kind of glob of positively charged matter in which negatively charged particles, which we now call electrons, were embedded. The conjecture, of course, was incorrect, and it was Thomson's own student, Ernest Rutherford, who showed that the positive part of the atom was concentrated in a central nucleus. However, Thomson's work had set the cat among the chickens!

Marie Curie

The end of the nineteenth century revealed scientific phenomena quite different from anything that had been experienced before. Physics, thus far, had made good progress in understanding mechanics, optics, electricity, magnetism, X-rays, the structure of the atom and radioactivity, which revealed a universe of new things that had to be grappled with. Madame Marie Curie was the indefatigable researcher who pursued the study of radioactivity and isolated radioactive elements, to set in motion the march into a new phase in the understanding of nature.

Marie Curie was born Marie Salomea Skłodowska in Poland in 1867, in a family of teachers. Her father was a teacher of mathematics and physics. When the Russian authorities, who were ruling Poland, decided to do away with laboratory instruction in the schools, Marie's father brought much of the laboratory from the school to the house. She did well in primary school and had to attend a clandestine institution for higher learning as women were not admitted in the regular schools. Marie and her sister helped each other to move to Paris for higher education and, in 1891, Marie reached Paris and enrolled in the University. There she met Pierre Curie, her future husband, and began work at the School for Physics and Chemistry, where he was an instructor. Marie did try to return to Poland, in 1894, but as women were still denied equal opportunities, she returned to Paris, where she and Pierre were married, while they both worked in science.

In the year 1895, Röntgen announced the discovery of X-rays. The next year, Antoine Henri Becquerel, a French engineer, in the course of looking for a link between phosphorescence and X-rays, discovered that salts of uranium emitted rays that were like X-rays in their penetrating power. Becquerel made this discovery while working with uranium salts, which are phosphorescent (things that glow in the dark if exposed to light for some time). By accident, he had left some of the salts on photographic plates and found that they affected the plates through a layer of paper, even without having been exposed to light. Hence, unlike X-rays or phosphorescence, these rays came from the uranium salts by themselves without any other external energetic agency. Furthermore, he found that pure uranium was even more powerful in its effects. This showed that the rays came from the uranium atoms and not as a result of any reaction. He also found that the rays from the salts, like X-rays, could discharge metal plates by getting the air between them to conduct electricity.

These discoveries were made just when Marie was working for her doctorate and she took uranium rays as the topic for her study. In the course of her work, she measured the strength of the radiation with the help of an instrument that Pierre Curie had developed to measure the strength of X-rays. She found that the strength depended on the quantity of uranium. And then, when working with pitchblende, which is the ore from which uranium is extracted, she found that the ore was even more radioactive (as the activity of these substances was called) than pure uranium!

This suggested that the ore contained something other than uranium—something that was even more radioactive than uranium. The Curies got to work to obtain quantities of uranium ore to refine. They found that they would need great quantities, indeed. At great personal cost, they obtained tonnes of the ore, which had to come from Austria, and spent long days and months in extracting the uranium. As expected, the ore from which uranium was extracted was more radioactive than the uranium extracted. This showed that there was another, strongly radioactive element in the ore.

For months, they went back to refining the residual ore. Finally, they extracted a bismuth compound, some 300 times more radioactive than uranium. But the compound appeared to be more radioactive than bismuth itself. They went back to the drudgery of refining the ore, and in 1898, they discovered a new element, which Marie Curie named 'polonium' after her native country. But there was still something to find. The Curies kept at work, and finally, at the end of the same year, they extracted another element, radium—a million times as radioactive as uranium!

Radium had all the properties of other radioactive elements and more. The radiation affected photo plates and got the air to conduct electricity. It even warmed simply by being left undisturbed and a large speck could also melt in this manner. The radiation made other substances phosphoresce and glow if just a little radium was mixed with them. Many tests and experiments were done. It was found that it affected living tissue and the radiation could kill small animals. The Curies even found that the radiation affected cancerous cells more readily than healthy cells and now radiation has grown to be an important weapon against cancer.

For the discovery, Pierre, Marie and Becquerel got the Nobel Prize for physics in 1903. The Curies went straight back to work to purify polonium and radium. Polonium was not difficult to extract, but radium was a challenge. A difficulty in refining radium is that it resembles barium, and pitchblende contains both metals. Finally, Marie Curie did purify radium, and in 1911, she received her second Nobel Prize, this time for chemistry.

Marie Curie became the first woman member of the École normale supérieure, the prestigious and exclusive French establishment of higher education. She also became the first woman professor of physics in the University of Paris. She headed the Radium Institute, a radioactivity laboratory of the Pasteur Institute, and the University of Paris, and she defined an international unit for radioactivity, which was later named the curie, in honour of herself and Pierre. She died in 1934, of a bone marrow ailment, considered to be the result of her exposure to radiation in the course of her researches.

Albert Abraham Michelson

The wave theory of light was the gateway to the understanding of the nature of matter. That light was an electromagnetic wave, the equivalence of mass and energy, and that the transfer of energy was not in a continuous stream but in packets, were the steps by which we reached the current state of knowledge. Researches into the speed of light were important guideposts along the way. Albert Abraham Michelson was an American physicist and the first American to win a Nobel Prize, who did some of the most important work in the field of study.

Michelson was born in 1852 in Strzelno, Poland, then part of Germany. But his parents moved to the U.S. when he was just two. He grew up in places along the western parts of the U.S. and obtained admission to the U.S. Naval Academy, which was being denied to him, by a protest to the U.S. President, when he was seventeen. At the Academy, he excelled in optics and drawing. After a short period of service in the U.S. Navy as a midshipman, he was posted to academic duties, and soon after, took leave to continue his studies in Europe.

Michelson was fascinated by methods to determine the speed of light. Many measurements had already been made and he could only improve or better the accuracy. Maxwell had calculated the speed of the electromagnetic wave, based on the electrical and magnetic properties of air or vacuum, and verifying and confirming it was a task that many undertook.

While Michelson later measured the speed of light with the best possible accuracy at the time, the experiment for which he is known was conducted in the years leading up to 1887. While light had been shown to be a wave, the understanding of waves was that they were the disturbances of some medium. For example, sound waves are disturbances of the air and waves in the sea are the movements of water. Electromagnetic waves, which passed through the vacuum of space, had also been considered to be the waves of an imaginary material: the ether. The question was: could the ether ever be detected? One view was that if there was ether, then the earth in its orbit around the sun, was passing through the ether at a speed of 30 km/second. Should there not be an 'ether wind', which would affect the speed of light in different directions?

Michelson had developed techniques for very fine measurements and believed he could look for signs of the ether, however feeble they may be. His instrument of choice was the interferometer. This was an arrangement where equality of distance was measured by the interference of waves of light from a common source, which had been split, sent on different paths and then brought together. If the two paths differed by a part of a wavelength, as opposed to a whole wavelength, the two beams would arrive out of step and this could be seen as an interference pattern. This is like the ocean waves that wash up at the beach interfering with the waves that are returning. When the waves meet in step, they rise high, but when they are out of step, they subside.

The Michelson interferometer is an arrangement of two paths of light at right angles, with mirrors at their ends to reflect a beam of light back. There is a half-silvered mirror, as shown in Figure 21, which splits a narrow beam of light into two and again brings the two beams of light together, to be sighted in the telescope. When the length of the two paths of light are the same, or differ by a whole number of wavelengths, the two parts of the split beam return in the same phase of vibration and there is a bright line, as the image of the slit through which the beam has started. If the lengths differ by anything but a multiple of the wavelength of light, however, the two beams arrive out of step, and they interfere. Like in the case of the waves at the seashore, what the telescope sees is a series of bright and dark fringes. If the beams are fully out of step, the central line is dark. A little off-centre, the path difference comes back in step, and we have a bright line. A little more off-centre, they are out of step again, and we have a dark line. The result is a series of dark and light fringes. If one of the mirrors is moved, so that the distance changes, the fringes are seen to move to one side, and the number of fringes that pass a cross-hair in the telescope would be a measure of the change in the distance. The arrangement is, hence, exceedingly sensitive and is able to measure lengths to the accuracy of the wavelength of light.

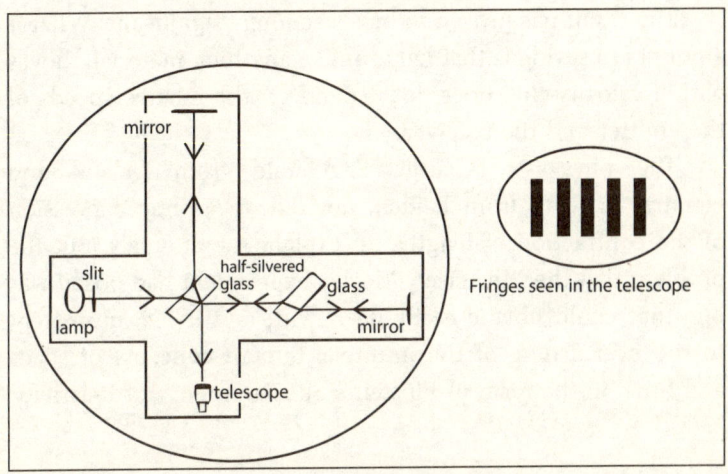

Figure 21

Coming back to whether there was ether, which may be the medium of light waves, one way to test was to look for the so-called ether wind. The arms of the interferometer could be set with one arm along the direction of the motion of the earth and the other at right angles. There would, hence, be a particular pattern of fringes. Now, if the interferometer were turned by 90°, the effect of the 'ether wind', if there were one, should switch from one arm to the other, and the interference fringes would shift position while the interferometer was turned.

Michelson, in collaboration with Edward Williams Morley, a skilled experimental scientist, carried out a series of trials in different combinations of conditions, in the day and night and at different seasons, and with the interferometer mounted on a slab that floated in a tub of mercury. But all the trials returned the same—the celebrated—negative result: there seemed to be no ether wind, and the speed of light seemed not to be affected by the movement of the earth!

The result has proved to be exceedingly significant. What it amounts to saying is that light, unlike anything material, moves with a velocity that does not depend on the relative speeds of the emitter and the receiver.

The physicists, George FitzGerald from Ireland and Hendrik Lorentz from Leiden, devised an ad-hoc expression of the contraction of lengths, to explain the anomaly. But the problem that the Michelson-Morley experiment had posed was one that could not be easily dealt with and it led, ultimately, to the overturning of the intuitive, human concepts of space and time, in the form of Einstein's Special Theory of Relativity.

Albert Einstein

The work of Albert Einstein in 1905 overturned some of the strongest convictions till that time about the physical world. The laws of Newton were shown to be only approximate, the nature of distance and time was redefined and the line between mass and energy was blurred. In a subsequent paper of 1915, Einstein reinterpreted the nature of gravitation in terms of the geometry of space.

Einstein was born in 1879 at Ulm, in the south of Germany. During his early years, he showed poor academic progress. Any adverse conclusion from this, of course, can be only of the method of education. However, he did later say that it was perhaps because he had not been given many answers, that he thought more deeply than others about time and space when he got down to it.

For all this, Einstein excelled in physics and mathematics and even as a young boy, had taught himself concepts far beyond his years. When he was seventeen, he enrolled in the Swiss Polytechnic School at Zurich for a four-year teaching diploma in mathematics and physics.

He qualified in 1900, but his teaching career was uneventful and short and, out of necessity, he joined the Zurich Patent Office where he examined applications for patents. His academic interests, however, were not interrupted. He had already formed some ideas about a mismatch between Newtonian mechanics and electromagnetic theory. At the Patent office too, he dealt with inventions dealing with the transmission of electrical signals, which are topics that occur in considerations that led Einstein to radical views about space and time—ideas which he later developed.

It was, however, a most productive period. In the year 1900, Einstein had published a paper on capillary effects in a leading journal. In 1905, he was awarded a PhD by Zurich University for his work on Brownian motion and molecular dimensions. This was also the year in which Einstein published his famous papers, one on the photoelectric effect, for which he received the Nobel Prize, and then, his famous work on Special Relativity.

The world of physics, at the turn of the century, was grappling with a contradiction. The bedrock of Galilean and Newtonian mechanics was that when a thing was projected from a moving platform, the speed of the platform added to the speed of the thing projected. In the case of light, however, this was found to be untrue. A beam of light, emitted by a source that was moving at whatever speed, still moved, whether forward or backward, at an unchanging speed. And again, the speed of light measured by a moving observer was the same as that measured by a stationary observer. The apparent anomaly had been highlighted by the celebrated Michelson-Morley experiment, which showed that the speed of light was the same in all directions, although the earth was hurtling through space at 30 km/second.

Einstein viewed the apparent anomaly in the way nature behaved as arising from ideas that had been derived from inaccurate experience of nature. Now, when we find that the speed of light stays the same regardless of the motion of the source or the observer, it is our ideas of space and time that needed to be modified. This, Einstein did, consistent with the speed of light (in a medium) staying invariant and holding that the laws of physics stayed the same for observers in uniform motion with respect to each other.

These conditions led to unusual, counter-intuitive conclusions. One was that lengths measured by a moving observer would shrink, compared to measurements made at rest. The other was that time passes slowly for a moving observer, compared to a stationary one. For example, if an observer in a train moving at a very high speed—a speed comparable to the speed of light—were to pass a station platform, the observer would measure the platform to be shorter than a surveyor at the station. And again, the time it takes for the train to cross the platform for the moving observer would be less than what a person at the station measures, for the reason that moving clocks run slower.

These differences, however, depend on how fast the relative motion is, and is undetectably small unless the speed is reasonably close to that of light. It is because the speeds of relative motion that we are familiar with are so much slower than that of light, that we have never noticed any of these effects. The effects, however, are undeniably there and have been verified in experiments. There is a class of elementary, subatomic particles, for instance, that have a certain rate of decay (or radioactivity) when they are at rest. The same particles, when they come down to the earth as high-speed cosmic rays, however, do not decay as much as they should in the time that we measure as the duration of their journey.

Another consequence of the theory is that the mass of a moving object is measured as greater than when it was at rest. The result is that as an object is moved faster and faster, it becomes heavier. The energy needed to increase its speed also increases, with the result that an object can never be made to go as fast as light. In this consequence of the Theory of Relativity lurks another concept: that there is an equivalence of mass and energy.

Einstein was able to derive a relationship of mass and energy, the famous $E = mc^2$ relation, which multiplies 'the mass' by 'the speed of light times the speed of light', to give the energy equivalent of the mass. This implies a great amount of energy for any reasonable mass, and this is the principle of nuclear power plants and the atom bomb.

After the epochal paper of 1905, Einstein went back to work on another idea about mass and energy that he found hidden in the principle of relativity. This was that gravity and acceleration are not distinct. We may experience momentary weightlessness when an elevator starts descending, or being weighed down for an instant when it starts ascending. Our own weight is, hence, only a sense of being accelerated. Combining this idea with the equivalence of mass and energy led, after some fiendish mathematics, to gravity being the effect that masses have on the curvature, not of a surface in space, but of space itself. Using this idea, Einstein was able to resolve a problem in the orbit of the planet, Mercury, which had not been possible by Newtonian mechanics.

One implication of Einstein's theory of gravitation was that light from a star that was hidden by the sun should still be visible, but for the glare of the sun, because light grazing past the sun should bend towards the observer (see Figure 22). Einstein published his paper in 1915, when World War I was in progress. Just after the war ended, in 1919, there was a total solar eclipse, where this prediction of the theory could be tested. The world of science was there, in strength, to observe the eclipse from South America and Africa, where it was total, and they did get a glimpse of stars from behind the sun's disk at the moment of totality!

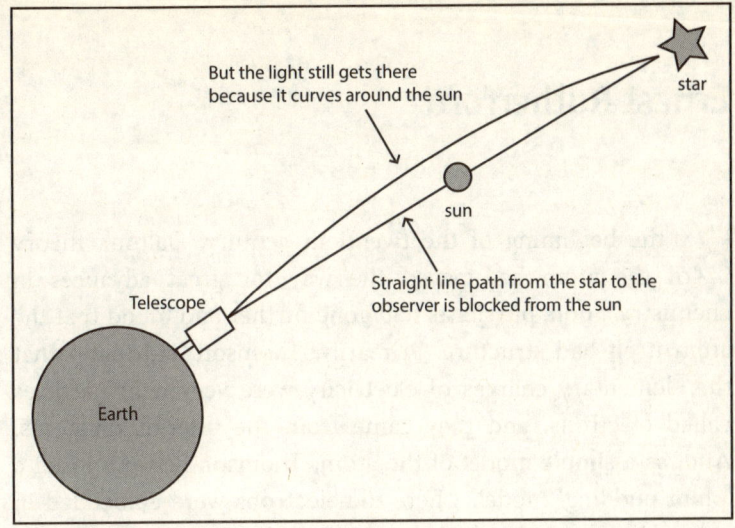

But the light still gets there
because it curves around the sun

star

sun

Straight line path from the star to the
observer is blocked from the sun

Telescope

Earth

Figure 22

Ernest Rutherford

By the beginning of the twentieth century, Dalton's theory of the atom had paved the way for great advances in chemistry. Soon, physicists had gone further and found that the atom itself had structure. Primarily, Thomson had found that the elementary charges of electricity were very light particles called electrons, and they came from the interior of atoms. And, as a simple model of the atom, Thomson had proposed a 'plum pudding' model, where the electrons were embedded in a spherical mass that had the positive charge to neutralize the electrons. Radioactivity had also been discovered and it was known that there were three kinds of radiation that was emitted when some atoms decayed.

It was Ernest Rutherford, a New Zealand-born British physicist, who analysed radioactive emission and probed the atom for the first glimpses, by inference, into this world beyond the reach of our senses.

Rutherford was born in 1871 at Brightwater, near Nelson, in New Zealand, to a farming couple that had migrated there from Essex, England. After bright and successful student years, and two years in research, he moved to England in 1891, to work in the Cavendish Laboratory, Cambridge.

He started work with Thomson, who had discovered the electron in 1897. The same year, Becquerel discovered radioactivity and Rutherford took this as a subject of study. He was able to identify two kinds of radiation, which were different from X-rays in their penetration power. Some years later, he analysed radioactive emissions using Thomson's method of measuring their deflection by magnetic and electrical fields and ways to count their numbers, and identified the two kinds of emissions. He found one kind, which he called alpha rays, to consist of positively charged particles that had four times the mass of the hydrogen atom. Rutherford subsequently showed that alpha particles were the doubly charged nuclei of the helium atom. The other kind of emission that he detected, the beta rays, consisted of negative particles, which were the same as electrons.

His analysis of radioactivity showed that there was a well-defined period of time in which any radioactive sample dropped to half its level of activity. This time—the half-life—is a characteristic of nuclei and is useful in the study of nuclear structure. The half-life has also found application in the dating of ancient artefacts, which contain radioactive materials that have been decaying since the time the artefacts were used.

After some years at Cavendish, Rutherford first moved to McGill University in Canada, then to the University of Manchester and finally returned to head Cavendish when Thomson retired. Over the years, he worked with many outstanding scientists and was responsible for the discovery of a number of new radioactive elements. He was awarded the Nobel Prize in Chemistry in 1908.

The most important contribution of Rutherford was the work he did from 1908 and 1913, with his collaborators, Hans Geiger and Ernest Marsden, where he used alpha particles as projectiles to investigate the internals of the atom. By the time these experiments were conducted, radioactivity had been fairly well studied and good sources of alpha particles were available. Rutherford used alpha particles emitted by radium bromide as a source and he used a gold foil as a target to be bombarded.

The purpose was to test the plum pudding model of the

atom that was current at the time. If the model were correct, an alpha particle would just fly through the atom. At the atomic scale, there would be no collision and rebound; the alpha particle would be affected only by the atom's electric fields. The distributed electrons would provide some uniform acceleration, but the positive charge, distributed over the volume of the atom, would exercise a low repulsive force.

The alpha particles passing through the gold foil were, hence, expected to be deflected very little, if at all. In the experiment, the stream of alpha particles was directed into the gold foil and the scattered stream on the other side was measured with the help of a fluorescent screen. While most of the alpha particles did fly through with almost no deflection, there was a good number that were deflected through large angles. Some alpha particles were even sent straight back!

The number of particles deflected through large angles was significant. This was simply not expected in the plum pudding model. Large deflections indicated there were concentrated centres of charge whose strong electric field affected the alpha particles that had been deflected. And the fact that the bulk of the alpha particles went through without deflection indicated that the bulk of the atom was empty space!

Although the experiment has been stated quite simply, it was complex in practice. For one, a concentrated stream of alpha particles had to be managed; for another, the container for the experiment had to be evacuated, so that the scattering by atoms of air, gas, or their products, would not interfere with the results. The experiment had to be done with alpha particles moving at different speeds and with different thicknesses of the scattering foil. All along, there had to be an arrangement to detect alpha particles deflected through all angles, all the way to 180°, or a full reversal of the projectile.

The first thing that Rutherford's experiment established was that the atom consisted of a concentration of charge at its centre (see Figure 23). It was not necessarily a positive charge, for a negative centre could also produce deflections through large angles. Rutherford, hence, carried out more experiments, of the scattering of alpha particles by different gases and finally proved that the results were clearly those of scattering by a positively charged centre.

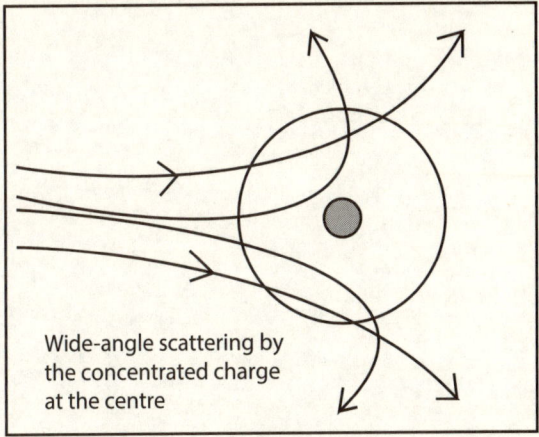

Wide-angle scattering by the concentrated charge at the centre

Figure 23

The finding now gave rise to considerations of how the electrons could stay distributed around a positive centre. Would they not be attracted and fall in? There was the suggestion that the electrons moved in orbits around the nucleus, like the planets around the sun. But this also could not be, because charges that moved in circles would radiate electromagnetic waves and soon crash into the centre. These were problems that had to be answered, but Rutherford had isolated one part of atomic structure and charted the course for more research.

Scattering experiments went on to prove more things, like the scattering by hydrogen often led to the centre of the hydrogen atom (which we now know to be the proton) being knocked out of the atom. When the scattering was by nitrogen, which has seven protons in its nucleus, a hydrogen nucleus got knocked out too, which changed the nature of the nitrogen nucleus. Along with research into the atom, Rutherford also set in motion the study of the nucleus, which occupied scientists for the rest of the century.

Max Planck

The march of physics hit a roadblock in the beginning of the twentieth century. Electricity, magnetism and electromagnetic waves had been understood, radioactivity had been discovered and so had the structure of the atom and the Theory of Relativity. But one phenomenon, seemingly less complex, resisted being explained. This was the manner in which the radiation from warm objects was distributed over the frequencies.

In the resolution of this problem, the German, Max Planck, discovered a feature of nature which shows itself at the very minute scale and is basic to the behaviour of matter in bulk. This one discovery changed the course of physics and led scientists to understand nature in ways that were earlier unimaginable.

At the turn of the nineteenth century, it was known that radiation from warm objects, mostly in the infra-red region of the spectrum, was distributed over a range of frequencies. It was also known that the warmer the object, the higher the frequency of peak radiation. An object that was just warm, for instance, would radiate only warmth, but a very hot iron would get 'red hot'. A mathematical expression, which described the distribution, however, was proving difficult to find.

As electromagnetic waves were known to arise from movement of electric charges, it was evident that radiation from warm objects arose from elementary oscillators within materials. Theories were, hence, built around radiation from vibrating atoms. Classical physics prescribes that in vibrating systems, the energy of vibration is equally distributed over different harmonics of vibration. As the higher harmonics are packed closer together, there is more energy in higher frequency bands. Different formulas were developed to express the observed strength of emission from warm objects but none proved satisfactory. One of the first laws was the Wien approximation, first derived by German physicist Wilhelm Wien in 1896. This predicted a steep rise in energy as one went up in the frequency, with a fall after the peak. The agreement was good at high frequencies, but not at the lower frequencies. A better law was Rayleigh's law and then the Rayleigh–Jeans law (co-developed with English physicist James Jeans). This was good at low frequencies but diverged at higher frequencies, implying very high energy at the highest frequencies.

It was left to Planck, in the year 1900, to break the impasse, by an epochal departure from the current understanding of waves, with a conjecture that energy was exchanged between the elementary oscillators of warm objects, not as a continuum but in discrete packets. This was pathbreaking and revolutionary, to say the least. There was not a scrap of evidence for such a thing, except that this was necessary for theory to fit facts about the radiation of energy from warm objects. The idea was not accepted at first, but it soon proved useful to explain many puzzling physical phenomena, and the burgeoning progress of physics that followed Planck through the twentieth century is based entirely on his one-step, counter-intuitive insight into the ways of nature.

Planck was born in 1858 in Kiel, northern Germany, the sixth child in a traditional, intellectual family. When he was nine, the family moved to Munich, where his teacher was a mathematician who taught him astronomy and mechanics, and gave him early grounding in the concepts of physics. Planck was gifted in music. He was a trained vocalist, proficient at the piano, organ and cello, and a composer too. But he was seized by physics. He went on to train in the subject at the University of Munich and then at Berlin, and qualified in 1880, with a dissertation in his chosen field of thermodynamics.

In 1894, while working as professor of theoretical physics at Humboldt University at Berlin, Planck received a commission to maximize the efficiency of light bulbs. The problem was essentially to find the distribution of light energy emitted at different frequencies by a filament at a given temperature, and generally, the frequency distribution of the emission from any warm body—ideally a 'black body', or one that only emits and absorbs all radiation—without reflection.

Planck analysed the problem from the principles of thermodynamics and the extent of disorder that would exist in a system of vibrators. From these principles, he arrived at a variation of Wien's law, known as the Wien–Planck law in 1899. This law, however, was found to be incorrect in its results and Planck revised his approach, to arrive, in October 1990, at a more satisfactory result. Within a month, he revisited the problem, from statistical principles underlying thermodynamics, and set down the law known as the Planck radiation formula.

Although the law was found to be accurate, Planck was not comfortable with the statistical and probabilistic bases of the work. He even confessed that he had taken recourse to them only to arrive at the result; not out of conviction. His methodology was based on thermodynamics and the belief in the transfer of energy, despite there being atomism in matter, was continuous. But he could see that the formula he had derived did not directly emerge from the bases of known physics. He reasoned that there, hence, had to be a departure from what was known.

He made this departure with the assumption (which seemed outlandish to many) that energy was transferred not continuously, but in steps, or packets called 'quanta'. The energy in radiation, he postulated, existed in discrete units, which depended on the frequency of the radiation, expressed as:

$$\text{Energy} = (\text{Planck's constant}) \times (\text{Frequency})$$

With this physical assumption, he could derive the same expression for the distribution of black body radiation and he announced this to the German Physical Society (Deutsche Physikalische Gesellschaft) in December 1990.

While there were many who did not, for some years, accept this apparent denial of the classical theory of electromagnetism, Planck himself believed, at first, that wave mechanics may be able to explain black body radiation without his device of considering that light moved in packets, which implied that light had a particle nature. The concept, however, set the world of physics on fire. Einstein used the idea to propose the photon—quantum of light—to explain the photoelectric effect. Niels Bohr explained the discrete frequencies of emission from the atom. A new science—quantum mechanics—was born to deal with interactions at the very minute scale where quantum effects become relevant, and of which the distribution of frequencies in black body radiation is a bulk manifestation.

It was a discovery that changed the landscape of physics, arising from a commitment that it is theory that needs to change, where needed, to accord with facts.

Niels Bohr

Thomson had shown that the atom contained lightweight, negatively charged electrons and Rutherford had shown that the positive charge of the atom was concentrated at the centre. Other researchers had seen that the light emitted from atoms was in characteristic frequencies, or narrow bands of colours, which were arranged in regular patterns. The current understanding, however, could not explain the stability of the atom or find a model to reconcile its features.

It was the Danish physicist, Niels Bohr, who brought in the idea of the quantum of energy and devised a model that exactly explained the pattern of emission frequencies. More details of the emission were found soon after, and though Bohr's model saw many improvements, the model has been the foundation for a century of development and remains basically unchanged.

Bohr was born in 1885 at Copenhagen, Denmark. He came from a well-qualified and academic family and was educated, till his master's and doctorate, in Copenhagen. In 1911, he got his doctorate with a thesis that studied the current theory of metals, which considered that electrons behaved like a gas. The theory, developed before the current detailed understanding of the atom, was clearly inadequate and that was exactly Bohr's conclusion. While his work, which was in Danish, was not well known, it brought out the shortcomings of the classical statistical treatment of the subject, as a forerunner of future work in the area.

Later in 1911, Bohr travelled to England and spent a year with Thomson who had discovered the electron, Rutherford who had showed that the positive charge of the atom was in its nucleus, and Charles Galton Darwin (grandson of Charles Darwin), who had worked on the role of electrons in the scattering of a beam of radioactivity by the nucleus of the atom. Bohr returned to Copenhagen in 1913 and went to work in the University of Copenhagen. It was then that he produced his three papers, called 'On the constitution of atoms and molecules', in three parts, and proposed the Bohr model of the atom.

The first model of the atom that had been proposed was the plum pudding model of Thomson: of a spherical mass of positive charge in which the smaller-sized electrons were embedded. This model was proved incorrect when Rutherford beamed positively charged particles at the atom. From the way the particles were scattered, he showed that the positive charge was concentrated at the centre of the atom. Hence, it appeared that the atom was a compact, positive centre, with electrons surrounding the centre, so that the atom was neutral, as a whole. The work of C.G. Darwin, who studied details of the scattering of particles by the nucleus, had suggested a manner of distribution of the electrons and there were theories of the electrons moving in orbits, like a planetary system. The emission of light by the atom could then be thought to arise from the electrons in a larger orbit dropping to a smaller one. The conceptual difficulty, however, was that moving electrons could not stay in orbit but would continuously radiate and crash into the nucleus. And then, the emission that came from atoms, unlike the radiation from a warm object, was not in all frequencies but at sharply defined wavelengths.

Another discovery, which contradicted the classical view, was that of Planck: that radiation was emitted by warm objects not as a continuous wave, but in discrete units, or packets of energy. These packets of energy were viewed as the differences in discrete steps in the energy levels of elementary oscillators. This theory—the quantum theory—had been used by Einstein to explain the photoelectric effect, which classical physics had not been able to explain.

Bohr saw that there was a parallel in the idea of discrete energy levels and the specific frequencies of radiation emitted by atoms. The patterns of emission were made to fit, by observers, into different formulas, which put out the series of frequencies when one or more integers appearing in the formula were changed. Although there was no theoretical basis for these formulas, a theory of the atom would need to express energy levels corresponding to integers, so that the series of emission lines that were observed could be explained.

Planck had proposed, in his theory, that the frequency of a packet of light was related to the energy of the packet by a simple relation:

$$E = h \times \nu$$

which is to say that the energy of the packet E is equal to 'a constant' times 'the frequency', with the constant being 'h', the Planck's constant, and ν being the frequency.

Bohr considered that an electron of an atom could be considered to be in any of a series of 'permitted' orbits, where the electron was not required to radiate electromagnetic waves. The frequency of the light emitted by an atom could then be taken as the difference in the energy of two permitted orbits, between which the electron transited, leading to the emission.

He then worked out the energy of the orbit of an electron, using the mechanics that worked for planetary motion and then added the condition that the energy would need to increase in steps, as determined by an integer in the formula. Once this condition, with an integer, was introduced, it became possible to arrive at a difference of two energy levels corresponding to different integers, and this difference tallied with the formulas that had been found to work.

This was a great success. It was a planetary model of the atom, as consisting of a positively charged core—the nucleus—surrounded by electrons moving in different orbits (see Figure 24). The quantum theory (that energy was transferred in packets) had been proposed as a departure from classical theory, in order to explain experimental results that contradicted classical theory. In the same way, the quantum principle was extended to the atom. Doing so correctly explained what was observed, and which classical theory had not been able to explain.

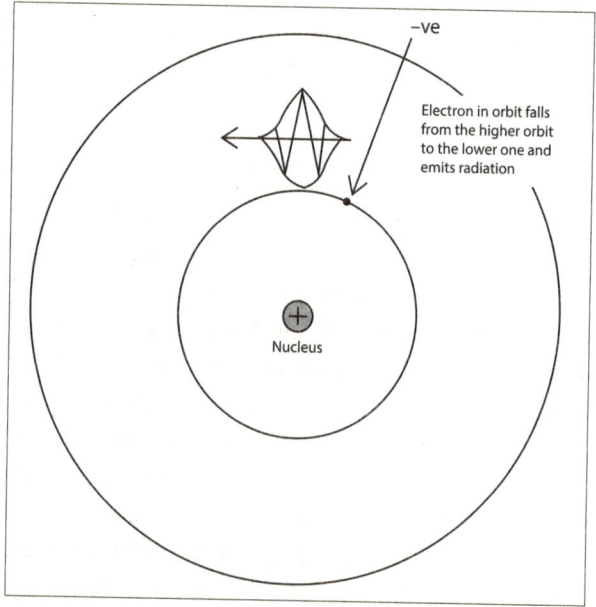

Figure 24

It was a breakthrough, no less. It worked well for the emissions of the hydrogen atom, which had only one electron in orbit, but not for atoms with more electrons. There were, hence, many refinements and modifications. But this was the first model, and even the refinements are, basically, forms of the first model. Bohr got the Nobel Prize for physics in 1922.

Alexander Fleming

Hygiene and antiseptics became part of hospitals and surgery in the mid-1800s. This led to drastic reduction of disease and mortality from injuries, or from surgery. Medical practice, however, was still powerless against a host of bacterial infections. It was the discovery of antibiotics, starting with penicillin by Alexander Fleming, in 1928, which transformed the control that we had over disease.

Fleming was born in 1881 in south-west Scotland. After secondary school in Scotland, he went to the Royal Polytechnic Institution at London. After working for a shipping firm for two years, he joined St Mary's Hospital and Medical School to qualify as a doctor when he was twenty-five. He continued as a research assistant and earned a degree in bacteriology. He stayed on at St Mary's till the beginning of World War I in 1914.

Right through the war, he was with the Royal Army Medical Corps, working in battlefield hospitals. He came back to St Mary's in 1918 when the war was over. Ten years later, he was appointed as professor of bacteriology in the University of London.

The use of antiseptics had made a great difference to wartime mortality. But what Fleming saw during the war was that antiseptics sometimes led to the death of a soldier who may have survived. He saw that while the antiseptic killed the harmful bacteria at the surface of the wound, the bacteria deeper within were out of reach. The antiseptic, however, also killed off the body's own mechanism of defence, which could have overcome the deeper bacteria. Fleming, hence, advised stopping antiseptics when they appeared to worsen the wound.

Back at St Mary's, he continued his study of antiseptics and found, by accident, that bodily secretions, like mucus, had a bactericidal effect. He isolated the active substance, lysozyme, and even found that it could be extracted in large quantities from egg whites. Lysozyme, however, was useful only against a small number of relatively harmless bacteria.

He continued his researches during his years at St Mary's and in 1927–28, while he was working on staphylococci—a group of bacteria that causes a brace of diseases—it so happened that he once left some cultures of the bacteria uncovered and unattended. When he returned, he found that a piece of common mould, or fungus, had fallen into one of the dishes. He noticed that the bacteria, in a circular patch around the piece of mould, had been destroyed. When he was reminded that something like this had happened with lysozyme too, he cultured the mould itself, and his tests showed that it produced a substance that was able to kill several disease-causing bacteria.

Fleming continued his study of the mould and identified it as belonging to the family, penicillium, a group of over 300 species of fungi. He carried out extensive tests with different bacteria and in varying conditions. What he found was that the substance that the mould released was effective against many bacteria, including those that caused scarlet fever, pneumonia, meningitis, diphtheria and gonorrhoea, but not typhoid or paratyphoid. Fleming gave this substance, which he had discovered, the name of penicillin and announced the discovery in the *Journal of Experimental Pathology*, in 1929.

The discovery, at first, appeared not to have great potential. It was difficult to obtain the mould in quantity and then to extract the active component. But it was undeniably effective against infections that had been considered fatal. And hence, soon after Fleming's first paper, by 1930, the use of antibiotics had become a practice in therapy, and research was actively undertaken. A team in Oxford worked out the molecular structure of penicillin. Howard Florey and Ernst Boris Chain at the Radcliffe Infirmary at Oxford found that even if treatment could not be continued in many cases due to a shortage of penicillin, the results of using penicillin were dramatic. They, hence, took on the challenge of finding ways to mass produce penicillin. At the start of World War II, it was recognized that penicillin had the potential to save lives in large numbers and the governments of the U.S. and Britain funded the research at Oxford. The result was that penicillin became available and was used extensively to treat Allied soldiers injured in the war. By 1945, there were stocks for public distribution.

More antibiotics were developed, and diseases for which there was no remedy till then, began to disappear. Life expectancy is said to have risen by eight years between 1944 and 1972. Better nutrition may be one reason, but the control of bacterial disease was the main factor.

Unlike the controversy over priority that mars many stories of scientific discovery, Fleming himself tried to deny his role and passed credit to Florey and Chain, for having transformed something only seen in a laboratory into an engine of saving millions of lives. But there is no denying the role of Fleming, not only in the discovery but in the continued lobbying, for years, with chemists and researchers to promote the production and application of penicillin. In 1945, the Nobel Prize for medicine was given jointly to Fleming, Florey and Chain.

Satyendra Nath Bose

The old problem, of the frequencies at which a warm body radiates heat, had been solved by Planck, and the offshoot—the quantum theory—was proving enormously successful. Planck had arrived at his formula by considering a warm body to be an assemblage of vibrators that were emitting and absorbing energy. By adding a condition that energy could be exchanged only in packets, or quanta of radiation, Planck had worked out a most probable distribution of net emitters, and this was the celebrated formula. Einstein went further, to derive the same formula from a different standpoint. He considered the cavity within a radiating object to contain a gas of photons, or the quanta of light. He then applied the principles of the well-understood gas laws, and came to Planck's formula with the help of Wien's law, a predecessor of Planck's law.

It is then that Satyendra Nath Bose, a young Indian physics teacher in the University of Dhaka, wrote a letter to Einstein, of which the following is an extract: 'I have ventured to send you the accompanying article for your perusal and opinion. You will see that I have tried to deduce the coefficient (...) in Planck's law independent of classical electrodynamics...'

The result was that Einstein himself translated Bose's article and had it published in *Zeitschrift fur Physik*, one of the most prestigious scientific journals. Then, Bose and Einstein, in collaboration, developed a vital principle of the behaviour of elementary particles of matter, which has guided the growth of physics ever since.

Bose was born in 1894 in Calcutta (now Kolkata), the eldest of seven children of an engineer in the East Indian Railway. After a brilliant school career, he completed his masters in physics from Calcutta University and started work at the Centre for Advanced Studies, for whose establishment he and some others had campaigned. In 1921, he was appointed as reader in physics at the University of Dhaka. It was at Dacca that Bose had studied Einstein's derivation of Planck's formula, and sent his hesitant letter to the master.

The method, while using statistical methods to look at the gas laws, is to consider that all molecules in a gas can have all possible energies, with the condition that the total energy has to stay the same. We can see immediately, that it is quite unlikely that just a few molecules would move at great speeds, while the others stay at low speeds, or vice versa. We can imagine that most of the molecules would be at some intermediate state. The way this works out mathematically is explained in the next paragraph.

Suppose there are two women and two men who shake hands with each other. We can see that each man has two women he can shake hands with, but only one man. Each woman, similarly, can shake hands with two men but only one woman. Among the six handshakes possible, there would, hence, be four man-woman handshakes and only two unisex handshakes. A random snapshot of this group of four is, thus, most likely to find them in man-woman handshakes. In the same way, of the different ways in which the energy of a quantity of gas can be distributed, the most likely turns out to be one in which there are the largest number of equivalent forms. This distribution, under different conditions of pressure, temperature and volume, turns out to change exactly according to the gas laws.

When Einstein arrived at Plank's law, he had considered

radiation in a cavity as a gas that consists of massless photons in place of molecules, but he also needed Wein's law to complete the exercise. Bose thought this was contrived. A reliable analysis should arrive at the correct result based on given facts alone. Else, it would be a restatement of the law or formula assumed, not a derivation of that law.

Bose analysed the problem in a different way. In the case of the four sociable men and women in the example given above, each person is, in principle, distinguishable; that is to say, each person can make out which of the two women or men he or she is shaking hands with, as the case may be. But photons are identical and cannot be told apart. Bose saw that this would make a difference. Take an example of a red and a blue ball being distributed in three compartments. This is possible in nine ways, like in Figure 25.

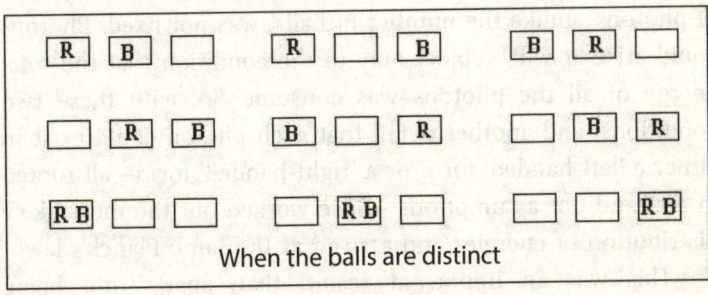

When the balls are distinct

Figure 25

But if the balls were the same colour, then the set of the first and the third, the second and the fifth, and the fourth and the sixth distributions become the same. Now, only six distributions are possible, like in Figure 26:

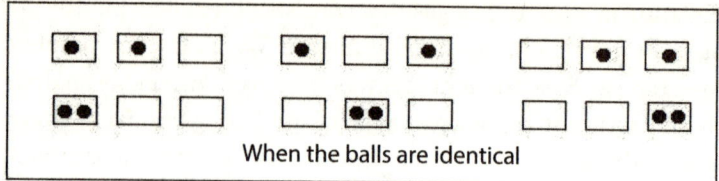
When the balls are identical

Figure 26

What Bose was doing was to work out a number for all the possible energy states that were possible in the container of the photon gas, something like the compartments in the example, and to see in how many ways the photons, like the balls in the above examples, could be distributed in the energy states. We can see that recognizing that the photons were identical was crucial.

Another thing that Bose provided for was that the number of photons, unlike the number of balls, was not fixed. Photons could arise at will, subject only to the condition that the total energy of all the photons was constant. So, with these two conditions, and another detail that each photon could exist in either a 'left-handed' form or a 'right-handed' form—all rooted in fact and not assumptions—Bose worked out the most likely distribution of energies and arrived at the same Planck's law!

This was an important result: that, apart from being considered packets or particles of energy, photons had to be treated like identical and indistinguishable entities!

Bose's paper, and the subsequent collaboration, set off a cascade of research worldwide. The idea of the quantum—a refinement in our thinking, which became significant only on very small dimensions—had barely taken root in the world of physics, but the concept alone had unseen depths, without the grasp of which it would have been of little utility. It was the insight that Bose introduced which enabled science to comprehend the mysteries of this unseen world in the following decades.

In recognition of Bose's fundamental contribution, the class of elementary, atom-scale, identical particles—like photons, the helium atom, the materials that display super-fluidity, or the celebrated Higgs boson—have been named bosons.

Edwin Hubble and Henrietta Swan Leavitt

Till as late as the early twentieth century, it was believed that the Milky Way—the galaxy that we see as a silver swathe across the sky on clear nights—was what the universe consisted of. The work of Edwin Hubble, using a device for estimating the distance of faraway objects, which was developed by Henrietta Swan Leavitt, showed that a multitude of stars and galaxies lay beyond the Milky Way. He also discovered a counter-intuitive feature of distant stars: that they were receding from us at feverish speeds, which grew faster as they moved further away.

The way a surveyor makes out distances is with the help of 'triangulation'. The object is sighted through a telescope, first from one place and again from a place shifted sideways by a few hundred metres. With the change in the direction of the telescope, the distance to a faraway object can be worked out by the mathematics of triangles. But this cannot work with distant stars because they are too far for even the orbit of the earth to make a difference. This is where the work of Leavitt provided a solution.

Leavitt was born in 1868, in Lancaster, Massachusetts. In 1893, as a graduate from Harvard University's Radcliffe College, an institute for women, she was engaged by the Harvard observatory for the task of classifying photographs. This was because women, at the time, were not allowed to operate the telescope. But in the course of her routine task, she discovered and established this remarkable relationship, as well as a scale to measure brightness, which has become the international standard.

Leavitt was working with photographic plates of stars in the observatory at Harvard College to catalogue the luminosity of stars. Now, this is merely a record of the luminosity. As luminosity depends both on the intrinsic brightness and the distance, we cannot reach a conclusion, either of how far the star is or how bright it is. But Leavitt, while working with a group of stars called Cepheid Variables, which show a pulsation of brightness, discovered that the rate of pulsation was related to the intrinsic brightness of the stars. Once there was a measure of the intrinsic brightness, it was a simple matter to use the apparent brightness to work out the distance of the star.

When Leavitt had established this principle, which is known as Leavitt's law, it became a routine practice for measuring the distance of an object, to discover the Cepheid Variables in the vicinity and then work out the distance.

Hubble was born in 1889 in Mansfield, Missouri, and was educated at the University of Chicago and then at Oxford. In acquiescence to his father's wishes, he studied law, but also took courses in astronomy and science. He finally came back to Chicago and got his PhD from the University's Yerkes Observatory in 1917.

In 1919, he joined the team working at Mount Wilson Observatory in California, which had the 100-in Hooker reflector, the world's most powerful telescope till 1949. With the help of the Hooker, Hubble identified Cepheid Variables in several spiralling collections of stars and during 1922–23, he proved, by application of Leavitt's Law, that these nebulae were too far away to be part of the Milky Way. His findings, which were at first widely opposed, showed that there were entire galaxies beyond our own, and they changed the whole approach to the astronomy of the distant universe.

Hubble's most important finding, however, was a relationship between the so-called red shift and the distance of a star, published in 1929. A feature of distant stars is that the frequency of the light received from the star reaches us with a shift towards the red side of the spectrum. This is identified by the shift in the position of the characteristic spectral lines of light emitted by the elements in the star. The implication of such a shift is that the star from which the light came is moving away from us at a speed high enough to affect the frequency of light. The effect is similar to the change in the pitch of a locomotive's whistle as it rushes towards us and speeds past. The whistle is shrill at first, when the locomotive is approaching, but falls in pitch as soon as the locomotive starts receding. In the same way, the light from a star that is approaching us would be blue-shifted, while a red shift indicates that the star is moving away.

But the discovery by Hubble was more than just a red shift. He found that the further away the star was from the earth, the greater the red shift. This means that distant stars are moving away from us and are going faster and faster as they move further away. In other words, the universe is expanding—and expanding at an accelerating speed!

This startling discovery set in motion widespread studies into the history of the universe. An expanding universe implies that sometime in the past, the universe was much smaller, and sufficiently in the distant past, the universe may have started from a single point! Theoretical models—of great confined energy leading to very rapid expansion with the production of elementary particles, radiation and finally matter in the form of hydrogen—of the primordial universe were constructed.

The expansion, described as 'from a point', is in fact removed from intuitive understanding, as it involves very high speeds and energy, calling for quantum mechanical and relativistic treatment. The scientist George Gamov, however, created a visual image of a great explosion, with the term 'big bang', to describe the beginning of the universe.

For a variety of reasons, the Nobel Committee was not able to decide on awarding the prize to Hubble during his lifetime. However, the National Aeronautics and Space Administration's space telescope, launched in 1990, which is in low orbit around the earth, was named the Hubble Space Telescope in honour of Hubble.

In fact, the idea that the universe may be expanding had been suggested by the Belgian astronomer, Georges Lemaître just before Hubble's experimental discovery. For this and other contributions to cosmology, the International Astronomical Union decided in October 2018, that the discovery, so far known as the Hubble law, be renamed the Hubble–Lemaître law.

Chandrashekhara Venkata Raman

In 1921, while returning by ship to India after a science congress in London, Chandrashekhara Venkata Raman was struck by the blue of the sea. The blue of the sky had been satisfactorily explained, but did the deep blue of the sea also have some secrets to be discovered?

Raman, Fellow of the Royal Society and Nobel laureate, was born in 1888 at Tiruchirappalli, in Tamil Nadu, India. After an outstanding early career, he entered the civil service at the age of nineteen, and was posted to Calcutta. Fortunately for the field of science, the Indian Association for the Cultivation of Science (IACS) fell on his way to work, and he regularly spent many hours there in study and research. His work attracted the attention of the Calcutta University and, in 1917, he was offered the position of professor in the department of physics.

The blue of the sky had been explained by the work of Lord Rayleigh as the scattering by molecules in the air, whose dimensions were smaller than the wavelength of light (see Figure 27). As per Rayleigh scattering, light of shorter wavelength—the light at the blue end of the spectrum—is scattered more strongly than light of longer wavelength—at the red end of the spectrum. A greater part of the blue component of sunlight is, thus, scattered by the atmosphere. This scattered light is again scattered back to the earth by other parts of the sky, and the sky looks blue. This is also the reason that the sun is reddish when low in the horizon, as the sunlight has been depleted of its blue content during its slanting passage through the atmosphere.

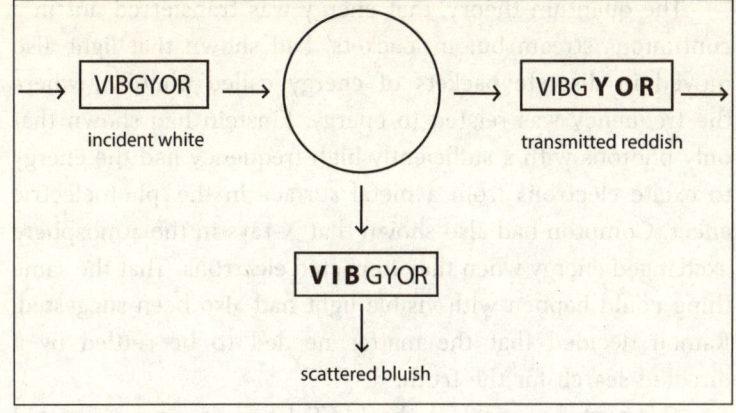

Figure 27

Raman wondered if liquids affected light in a similar way. The question soon led to investigation that revealed a faint effect on light, now known as the Raman Effect. While the Rayleigh scattering only separates the components of incident light by dispersing some wavelengths more than others, in the Raman Effect, a single wavelength of light that falls on molecules bounces off at a slightly changed (that is, a shorter or longer) wavelength. This change in the wavelength is related to the nature of the molecules involved and the Raman Effect has become an important tool for investigating the structure of molecules.

Getting back to the scattering of light by liquids, the work done till then was not better than some refinement of work done with air. A thought crossed Raman's mind that the 'quantum' effects of energy getting expressed as waves may play a role in scattering. The Rayleigh theory of scattering, which was developed before quantum effects were known, was a showpiece of the classical theory of waves. But recent discoveries had shown that light also displayed a 'particle' character.

The quantum theory, that energy was transferred not in a continuous stream but in 'packets', had shown that light also moved in discrete packets of energy called photons, where the frequency was related to energy. Einstein had shown that only photons with a sufficiently high frequency had the energy to excite electrons from a metal surface in the 'photoelectric effect'. Compton had also shown that X-rays in the atmosphere exchanged energy when they impacted electrons. That the same thing could happen with visible light had also been suggested. Raman decided that the matter needed to be settled by a directed search for the truth.

The next few years at the IACS laboratory were devoted entirely to the scattering of light by liquids. IACS then had some brilliant students and a good bit of data was generated. The experimental setup required a source of intense, white light. This was provided by directing the sun's rays into the lab with the help of a mirror. This light was passed through a violet filter and then channelled to pass through the liquid being studied. With the liquid illuminated in this way, the light scattered at right angles was examined by viewing the liquid from the side, with a telescope.

While it was natural that the scattered light would have a violet part, the idea was to peer through filters of other colours to see if the scattered light contained other components. The scattered light was extremely feeble and any light of colours other than violet would have been even feebler. The incident beam was derived from bright sunlight and the observers were young persons who had been confined to a darkened cubicle for an hour before the experiment was started. This was to prime the observers' eyes to maximum sensitivity and the box in the IACS laboratory was facetiously called the 'black hole of Calcutta'.

As the experiment progressed, evidence began to collect that the scattered light contained a 'modified' colour. But how could this be? There was no hint of this in Rayleigh's theory. Could it be a case of fluorescence, where atoms absorb light, consume some energy internally and then emit light of a lower frequency? Raman had to be sure. His team repeated the trials with the greatest purity and with fifty different liquids. But in every case, the observations were the same. Could it be fluorescence every time?

Yet another observation was that the 'modified' part of the scattered light was 'polarized'. Polarization is a special feature of light waves. The particles of water in ripples on a pond move up and down. With a light wave, however, there is no sense of 'up and down'. The movement of the electromagnetic field can be in any plane, up-down, left-right or slanting. The light, where the plane of vibration has nevertheless been constrained to one plane, is called polarized light. Raman found that the modified scattered light, like all scattered light, was polarized. But polarization was not a feature in fluorescence. This proved that the 'modified' light was a real 'visible light Compton effect'! (See Figure 28).

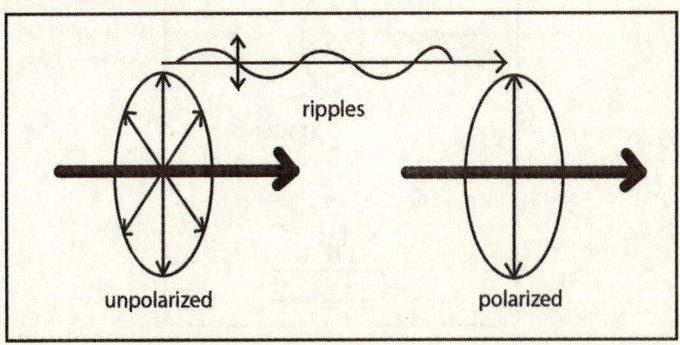

Figure 28

A final test was using incident light of sunlight and a filter of uranium glass, which allows only a very narrow wavelength band, with a thin line of the spectrum, to pass. The scattered light was then viewed, not with a telescope, but with a spectroscope, an instrument with a prism that separates the colours of light. Now, the result was one with a distinct feature. The scattered light was of the same colour as incident light, and also a faint narrow line of a lower frequency! (See Figure 29).

It was a sensational discovery, which Raman published at once. He also published the explanation: that the incident 'photon' had transferred some of its energy to the molecule and was thus left with less energy. The exchange was in a quantum of energy, which is why there was a gap between the lines. Moreover, Planck's relation connected the wavelength of a photon with its energy. It was a dramatic verification of the quantum theory and an instance of a molecule absorbing a definite amount of energy. Raman spectroscopy now deals with both absorption of energy from the photon and transfer of energy to the photon, and is used to investigate the sensitive details of molecular structure.

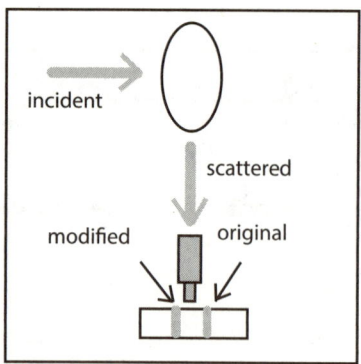

Figure 29

Recognition was fast in coming. Rutherford announced the discovery in the Royal Society, the British Government conferred a knighthood and in 1930, Raman became the first Nobel laureate in science outside Europe and the U.S.!

Subrahmanyan Chandrashekhar

If it was in a ship from England to India where C.V. Raman conceived his greatest work, it was aboard a ship on the way to England, in 1930, that the Indian scientist, Subrahmanyan Chandrashekhar carried out much of the preparatory work for his discovery some years later—that the fate of larger stars was to end up as black holes. The black hole, a region of space from which gravitational forces do not allow even light to escape, is one of the most spectacular icons of modern astrophysics.

Chandrashekhar, Fellow of the Royal Society and a Nobel laureate, was born in 1910 in Lahore, then part of British India. He was from an illustrious Indian Tamil family (C.V. Raman was his uncle), and he completed his education in Chennai. Even as an undergraduate, he had learnt much of both the new quantum mechanics (which applies at the scale of the very small), as well as Einstein's General Theory of Relativity (which applies at the scale of stars and galaxies). At the age of twenty, he was on his way to England for further studies.

The origin of stars, as then understood, was that they form when clouds of gas are drawn together by the forces of gravity. As the cloud gathers together, it warms, like the air in a bicycle pump when it is compressed. The temperature rises to millions of degrees, which starts nuclear reactions: that of hydrogen nuclei combining to form helium. This again increases the pressure, which overcomes the force of gravity. The cloud then expands, till the fuel for the first nuclear reactions runs out. When this happens, gravity takes over to set off more energetic nuclear reactions and the creation of heavier elements. This leads to expansion, followed by compression, and so on.

After several cycles, all the nuclear fuel is spent. Now there is nothing to counter gravity and the star collapses. It gets smaller and the force of gravity at the surface gets stronger. But does the star get smaller without limit and reduce to a point? What would be the density of matter in the star so compressed? Is this the fate of a star—to ultimately disappear?

Fortunately, the collapsing star is saved from such ignominy by the quantum theory. The wave nature of matter introduces a 'spread' in the dimension of anything and places a limit on how small a thing can get. This condition, when things get compressed very close together, gives rise to a pressure that does not depend on temperature. This pressure keeps things from getting any smaller, and this is the final state of a star.

The question of what happens to a star that collapses took a firm hold on Chandrashekhar, and during the two weeks of the voyage, he applied himself to see what he could make of it. An early stage in the evolution of stars, post expansion, is when they are vast and cool, and known as 'red giants'. After some cycles of expansion and compression, when they have no nuclear fuel for further expansion, heavier stars collapse under gravity to crush their very atoms into neutrons. As neutrons do not mutually repel, a neutron star collapses till it is the densest kind of matter known. Many of them radiate heat and light. Small and bright stars like this were discovered, and they were called 'white dwarfs'.

The subject of Chandrashekhar's interest was what happened within a white dwarf. The data about white dwarfs, at the time, was only what could be seen through the telescope and deduced by spectroscopy. What was going on inside the star had to be conjectured in theory. One fact that could be imagined was the state of the atoms in a white dwarf. Unlike normal atoms, with a positive centre surrounded by electrons, powerful collisions in a white dwarf would separate the charges and create a gas of charged particles. There would be huge forces of attraction and repulsion, and energy would be distributed among the particles according to the rules of quantum mechanics.

During the voyage to England, Chandrashekhar worked out how things should be within the white dwarf and came up with a solution that bristled with problems. In the case of a white dwarf of low mass, the equations behaved well and provided solutions that fit the data. But when the mass of the star increased beyond a point, the equations displayed features that did not make sense!

In England, Chandrashekhar worked under the best names of the time, got his doctorate, and then a position in Trinity College, Cambridge. He had discussed white dwarfs with his guide, Professor William A. Fowler, and continued to work on the problem. He came up with a new formulation, where he considered that the speeds of the particles in a collapsed star would be comparable to the speed of light. The rules of Einstein's Theory of Relativity would then need to be applied. When he carried out this exercise, the result had important differences from earlier results. When the density was low, the new results agreed with the earlier ones. To get a quick peek at what would happen when the density was increased, Chandrashekhar considered the case of infinite density. This condition, he found, did change the way the parameters of the star were related, but it still allowed the white dwarf to exist if it had a mass of about 1.4 times that of the sun. But there was something of a shock: if a star with a mass 1.4 times that of the sun should run out of fuel, it would shrink to a point!

Chandrashekhar worked on this result for months and

presented it to many illustrious men of science. Einstein's General Theory held that gravity and acceleration being indistinguishable, the presence of a mass would distort space itself, so that another mass experienced a force. It had been shown that the mass of the sun could bend rays of light so that the stars that were blocked out became visible during an eclipse. Karl Schwarzschild, a German physicist, had worked it out that a sufficiently large mass would distort space so that light from the mass could not escape. Had Chandrashekhar's white dwarf reached the Schwarzschild radius? For years, nobody was willing to think it possible. There was ridicule and a celebrated senior scientist lashed out at the young Indian scientist. There were comments like, 'I think there should be a law of nature to prevent a star from behaving in this absurd way', which was hardly a riposte to cold mathematics!

Chandrashekhar decided not to beat his head against a wall. He put down his findings in a book and moved on to other fields of research. He worked in different areas, every time leaving an indelible mark. But the book on collapsed stars, written in 1937, continued to smoulder, while evidence of the evolution of stars accumulated. At first, neutron stars were discovered. Then, in 1971, when observations of X-rays were made from outside the atmosphere, what may be a black hole was inferred. Since then, evidence has mounted and the work that Chandrashekhar did in the 1930s has become the basis of a vast field of theoretical and experimental astrophysics.

Recognition had already come to Chandrashekhar for other work that he had done, and in 1983, he was awarded the Nobel Prize for his work on collapsed stars, with Fowler. In 1998, as the result of a contest that drew over 6,000 entries worldwide, NASA's Advanced X-ray Astrophysics Facility, still in orbit around the earth, was renamed the Chandra X-ray Observatory.

Werner Heisenberg

During the early years of the twentieth century, with new discoveries—like radioactivity, the electron and the nucleus, the structure of the atom, the Theory of Relativity, the concept of the quantum of energy, the photon and the wave nature of light—the essentials of laws and principles of physics were reformulated. Matter was seen to move and interact in the form of a wave, and waves were found to transfer energy and momentum like a material thing. A new form of mechanics, which would account for both kinds of behaviour, was hence required. German physicist Werner Heisenberg was one of the architects of this new manner of approaching the physics of small dimensions.

With the discovery of lightweight, negatively charged electrons, and the positively charged centre of an atom, the atom's structure was likened to the solar system, with electrons in orbits around an attracting, central nucleus. The model now had to explain how the atom emitted photons of light only in specific frequencies. The quantum concept—that energy was transferred in packets—was, hence, built into the model, to limit the radii of orbits that electrons were permitted to occupy. Emission from the atoms was then explained as release of energy when an electron transited from a higher energy orbit to a lower energy, with the frequency corresponding to the difference in energy.

The community of physicists applied themselves to find a mathematical construct that would deal at the same time with waves and particles, and include the special conditions for specific, 'permitted' orbits in the atom. The implications of the mathematics that was involved, and the results of experiments, were being assessed to build a self-consistent theory. This was the stage during the 1920s—a period during which much of the theoretical bases of quantum mechanics were being discovered—when Heisenberg entered the scene, and brought with him the insight that enabled the strides of progress that followed.

Heisenberg was born in 1901, the son of a scholar of classical languages, in Würzburg, Germany. After early education in Munich, he joined Munich University, where he trained under Sommerfeld and Wein. After he received his PhD, he moved to Gottingen to work with Max Born. In 1926, he was appointed lecturer in theoretical physics in the University of Copenhagen and the next year, as professor at Leipzig.

Although Heisenberg went to many higher places in later years, he is best known for the work he did between 1924 and 1927. In 1925, at just twenty-four years of age, Heisenberg turned out a paper that tried to untie the knots in the current work in quantum mechanics. Rather than speak of the orbit of the electron and its radius, which were things that could not be observed or measured, we need to speak, he said, of the intensities of the frequencies emitted by an atom, which is what we can measure. With each frequency, Heisenberg associated two numbers—the respective energy levels—and then, with a series of mathematical steps, he worked out rules to compute intensities.

Although it was not thus expressed, the format of computation that Heisenberg devised amounted specifically to a mathematical procedure known as 'matrix multiplication'. Matrices are arrays of numbers, with rows and columns. When the number of columns of one matrix is the same as the number of rows of another, the matrices can be multiplied, as shown in Figure 30. We can see that the result matrix has as many columns as the first matrix has rows, and as many rows as the second matrix has columns. When the number of rows and columns is the same, multiplication is also possible the other way around. But when we do this, we find that the result is not the same! This amounts to saying that A x B is not the same as B x A. This was a quality that Heisenberg's method shared with matrices. Heisenberg's famous paper of 1925 does not speak of matrices, but it is a scheme by which the intensities of the frequencies at which the hydrogen atom would emit radiation could be calculated.

$$\begin{bmatrix} a & b \\ c & d \end{bmatrix} \times \begin{bmatrix} u & v \\ w & x \end{bmatrix} = \begin{bmatrix} au+bw & av+bx \\ cu+dw & cv+dx \end{bmatrix}$$

The product of a pair of 2×2 matrices is another 2×2 matrix, according to the scheme that is shown. However, if we switch the order of multiplicands, we get a different result.

$$\begin{bmatrix} u & v \\ w & x \end{bmatrix} \times \begin{bmatrix} a & b \\ c & d \end{bmatrix} = \begin{bmatrix} ua+vc & ub+vd \\ wa+xc & wb+xd \end{bmatrix}$$

Figure 30

This method, which came to be known as 'matrix mechanics', was taken up by leaders of quantum mechanics, Max Born and Paul Dirac, and paved the way for other researchers to discover new and illuminating secrets of the quantum world.

The other and better-known insight that Heisenberg contributed to science was in 1927—the uncertainty principle. With the wave nature of a particle and the probabilistic nature of outcomes in the quantum world, there is always a fuzziness, or 'spread', in the position of a particle. Heisenberg showed that this uncertainty of position had nothing to do with the method of measurement, but was intrinsic. Moreover, it was related to the uncertainty in the momentum, or the product of the mass and the speed of things. Where there was uncertainty in the momentum, it was possible to get close to the location, but if we fix the momentum then the location becomes uncertain.

For example, let us locate an electron that is at rest. The only way to locate the electron is to see it, by detecting a photon that strikes the electron and comes under our microscope. When this happens, we know its position with certainty, but the photon, in bouncing off the electron, has transferred momentum to the electron and set it in motion. One way to limit the uncertainty is to use a microscope with a small objective lens, so that we know the path of the photon. But a small objective lens would reduce the resolution of the microscope and make the position uncertain. Another way is to reduce the recoil of the electron by using low frequency light. But this, again, leads to a low resolution of the image (see Figure 31).

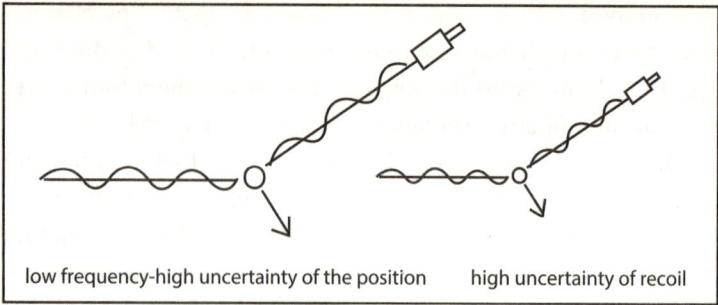

low frequency-high uncertainty of the position   high uncertainty of recoil

Figure 31

Heisenberg's working, in fact, shows that the mutual compensation of uncertainty in pairs like position and momentum, or energy and time, is a part of nature and measurements are always a trade-off. The implications are extensive and have guided all subsequent understanding.

Einstein was quick to recognize the value of the work done and the very next year, in 1928, he nominated Heisenberg for the Nobel Prize, who was awarded the same in 1932, for 'the creation of quantum mechanics' and its application.

Erwin Schrödinger

The understanding of physics underwent a fundamental change after the discoveries of the Curies, Thomson, Planck, Einstein, Rutherford and Bohr. Traditional physics was limited to the visible universe of ordinary experience. In the new physics, there was a submicroscopic world where the known laws of physics had to modified and refined. These, in fact, were the correct laws and the classical laws were approximations.

There were, however, no clear rules, like Newton's laws, to solve a dynamical problem at the level where quantum effects were relevant. These were developed over the later decades of the twentieth century by a succession of scientists. While Heisenberg made valuable contributions, an equal contemporary was Erwin Schrödinger, who gave the world a mathematical equation to calculate at the atomic level, in the same way as in classical physics.

Schrödinger was born in 1887 in Vienna, Austria, to a family with some academic tradition. He was educated at Vienna and worked his way through academia in Vienna (Austria), Stuttgart (Germany), Wroclaw (Poland), Zurich (Switzerland), Oxford (England), Princeton (U.S.), Ghent (Belgium) and Dublin (Ireland). Till 1920, Schrödinger carried out notable theoretical and experimental work in a large number of areas in physics. In later years, however, he was primarily a theoretician.

By the 1920s, the ideas of the quantum, the particle nature of light and the wave nature of matter had progressed and so had ideas about the atom. German physicist Arnold Sommerfeld had developed a relativistic version of Bohr's planetary model of the atom. Experiments had shown that the spectral lines of atoms could split into a 'fine structure' under a magnetic field. Against the single 'quantum number', which, in the Bohr model, was the order of the orbit of an electron around the nucleus, Sommerfeld introduced more numbers to select variations of orbits and explain fine structure. Swiss-American physicist Wolfgang Pauli introduced the idea of an intrinsic spin in the electron and a rule that two electrons in one orbit must have a different 'spin'. New problems, other than those of atomic structure, (for instance, the scattering of neutrons by the nucleus) had been approached using quantum principles.

Schrödinger made important contributions in the development of the theory. He observed certain geometric features that the orbits of electrons had, which helped develop a merger of wave theory and mechanics, as the subject of wave mechanics. With the inclusion of quantum principles and the wave-particle duality, Schrödinger saw that a physical system, like a particle moving in a force field (a pendulum swinging under gravity would be a readily comprehensible, but classical, example), could be represented by a mathematical expression called a wave function. The energy of the system could then be represented by an operator, which would act on the wave function, and, if some conditions were satisfied, the action of the operator would throw out the whole-number multipliers of the energy that the system could take.

The equation, which is known as the Schrödinger equation, can be written as:

$$H\Psi = E\,\Psi$$

where H is the operator related to the total energy of the system, which acts on Ψ, the wave function.

In the cases where the equation applies, the result is a 'number' times 'the same wave function', and the values that E can take are the energy levels that the system can have.

This equation, in fact, is the quantum mechanical parallel of Newton's Law, F = mA (acceleration A, of a body of mass m, depends on the force F). Newton's equation helps us work out, for instance, how fast a stone would be moving some time, say five seconds, after it has been dropped under gravity. In the same way, Schrödinger's equations (for there is another form: the 'time dependent' equation) allows us to follow the progress of a quantum mechanical system.

Schrödinger worked on this formulation and refined it to make it mathematically more tractable and applied it to many problems, like the oscillator, the rotator and the diatomic molecule. With further refinement, the equation could handle the problem of neutron scattering too. Then, there were more refinements, with which the Schrödinger equation could deal with all of wave mechanics.

Schrödinger took the early steps towards the physical interpretation of the wave function. In the case of the electron, he viewed the function as the density of the charge smeared across the field. This interpretation was later refined as the value of the wave function of a particle, at a point, being related to the probability of the particle being detected at that point. In the case of a system, this would be the probability of the system being in a particular state. With this interpretation, quantum mechanics regards a system, when left alone, as existing in a combination of all its possible states. When a measurement is made, it falls into one of the states and yields that value to the measurement, with a given probability that it would fall into any one of the possible states.

This possibility of a system to be in many states at once

explains a number of otherwise surprising phenomena. For instance, when a wave of light passes through a pair of slits and falls on a screen, the interference of waves that come to the screen from the two slits would create a pattern of light and dark fringes. If this is done with a stream of electrons, again, we have a fringe pattern, because the electrons also behave like waves. In this case, the interpretation is that each electron passes through both slits at once. However, if a sensor is placed at the slits to detect which slit the electrons passed through, the 'coherent' state of passing through both slits is destroyed and so are the fringes (see Figure 32).

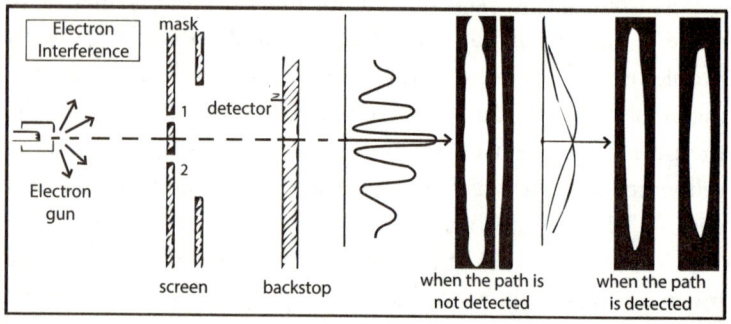

Figure 32

Schrödinger's equation made it possible to analyse different systems, like atoms, molecules, properties of solids, fluid motion, interactions, radioactive decay, etc. It was a development that made quantum mechanics become a regular part of the physicist's toolkit. In 1933, Schrödinger was awarded the Nobel Prize in physics for his work.

Schrödinger, as a young man, had been influenced by the philosopher Arthur Schopenhauer, and, though himself an atheist, was interested in ancient and oriental religions. His father was an amateur botanist and Schrödinger was an admirer of Charles Darwin and the 'origin' of species. In his lecture series, 'What is life', which he delivered during his stay in Dublin, he examined how processes in living cells could be accounted for in physics and chemistry. A concept by him, of the 'aperiodic crystal' containing information about the chemical bonds in its structure, was acknowledged by molecular biologists Francis Crick and James Watson, who discovered the DNA, as having been an inspiration to seek such a structure in biology.

Francis Crick, James Watson and Maurice Wilkins

Mendel, in the 1860s, had discovered that the offspring of pea plants, where one parent had white flowers and the other had purple flowers, would have white or purple flowers and not flowers of a colour in between. The discovery was that heredity happened in units, which he named 'factors', each of which corresponded to a trait, like the colour of flowers in pea plants. Mendel identified the factors as recessive or dominant, and developed rules of how they appeared in the generations. The mechanism by which this came about, however, was not known. It was after a chain of discoveries over nearly a century, that the double-helix structure of the DNA molecule and its role in heredity were discovered in 1953.

During the 1880s, Theodor Boveri, a German biologist, identified chromosomes (thread-like structures found in cells) as the means by which heredity was transferred between generations. At the turn of the century, there was a revival of the findings of Mendel, and Boveri saw a connection between Mendel's rules of inheritance and the behaviour of chromosomes. American geneticist Walter Sutton worked on the idea, which grew into the Boveri–Sutton chromosome theory.

In the meantime, in 1869, Friedrich Miescher, a Swiss scientist, had discovered a molecule—nuclein—in the nuclei of cells. He found nuclein was different from the proteins that he was looking for, and that it contained hydrogen, oxygen, nitrogen and phosphorus, with a unique ratio of nitrogen to phosphorus. Nuclein was later named 'nucleic acid', and then 'deoxyribonucleic acid', or DNA.

During the early 1900s, it was discovered that the DNA molecule consisted of a 'backbone' chain, with branches of just four chemical groups called 'A', 'G', 'C' and 'T'. The process of heredity, however, was not associated with DNA, as it was believed that proteins were more likely the carriers. It was a discovery by Frederick Griffith, an English army doctor, which turned the tide.

In 1928, Dr Griffith was trying to find a vaccine for the pneumonia bacterium. There are two strains of the bacterium, 'R', the harmful kind, and 'S', which causes no disease. When Griffith injected a mouse with R, it resulted in disease, but not when the S strain was injected. When he injected the R strain that had been neutralized with heat, again there was no disease. But when he injected the dead R strain with the harmless, living S strain, it resulted in disease. It looked like the genetic material of the dead bacteria had changed the nature of the harmless strain!

Years later, in 1944, Oswald Avery, at the Rockefeller University, New York, could confirm Griffith's discovery and isolate the part of the DNA of the bacteria that could transfer disease. This was proof that it was the DNA and not protein that carried genetic information. A further proof was that when a protein-digesting enzyme was added, the injected material still caused disease. But when an enzyme that damaged the DNA was added, there was no disease.

Another milestone in the discovery of DNA structure was by Erwin Chargaff, an Austro-Hungarian biochemist, who did most of his work in Columbia University. Chargaff discovered that of the units, A, G, C and T found in DNA, the number of units of G was the same as of C and the number of units of A was the same as of T. This was an observation that strongly hinted at a structure where G and C were paired, as were A and T. It was a hint that was soon picked up by James Watson and Francis Crick.

Watson was born in 1928 in Chicago and went to the University of Chicago, Indiana University and the University of Copenhagen, and later, worked in the Cavendish Laboratory at Cambridge. Crick was born in 1916 in a village near Northampton in England. He was exposed to science even as a boy and had a successful student career through University College, London, and was an Honorary Fellow of Gonville and Caius College, Cambridge, before he reached Cavendish Laboratory.

The first definitive step in nailing down the structure of the DNA was taken by Rosalind Franklin at Cambridge. Franklin was born in London in 1920 and had an uphill task as a woman scientist. Nevertheless, she mastered the field of X-ray crystallography and in 1951, she was able to get a pair of images representing two strands of DNA, which suggested a helical structure.

When she presented her results at a lecture in King's College, Watson, from the Cavendish Laboratory, was there. He and his colleague, Crick, had been working on the DNA structure. Franklin's X-ray images, which her colleague, Maurice Wilkins, showed Watson and Crick, confirmed the structure that they had proposed. Both Franklin and Wilkins, and Watson and Crick, published the X-ray images and the paper on DNA structure in the same issue of the journal, *Nature*, in 1953.

The model that Watson and Crick theorized for the DNA molecules was that of a pair of strands, each with a backbone of a sugar and phosphate, with side chains of the four groups, C, G, A and T (see Figure 33). The two strands wind around each other in the form of reverse spirals, and the groups, C, G, A and T, form links with each other, like the rungs of a spiralling ladder. There is a rule that C and G will form links only with each other and that A and T, in turn, with each other. Thus, given a sequence of the four groups, in any order, in one strand, the sequence on the other strand is the complementary sequence formed by matching side chains.

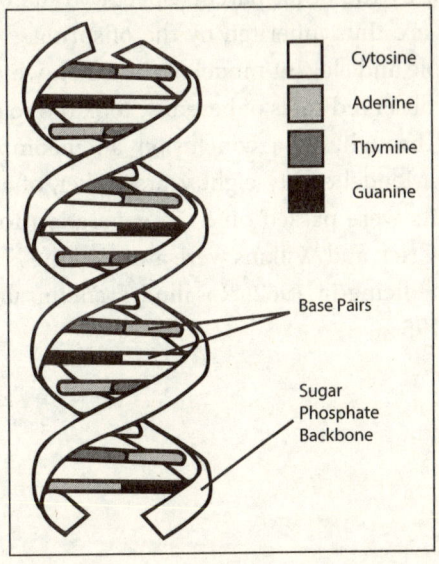

Figure 33

This structure has a powerful consequence. It implies that if the two strands of the DNA should get separated, each strand could regenerate its partner from a chemical pool, because each G, C, A or T would connect only with a C, G, T or A, respectively. The side chains would then form the successive sugar-phosphate links and recreate the second strand of the double helix.

This is, in fact, the mechanism of reproduction. When a cell is ready to divide, the DNA lines up and splits into two. Each half enters the daughter cells, and there, they reform their complementary strands for the daughter cells to become full-fledged cells. As the DNA is faithfully copied, the generations of cells inherit the traits of the parents. In the case of sexual reproduction, half the DNA is contributed by one parent and the other half by the other parent. Specific traits of one or the other parent are thus inherited by the offspring.

This simple and elegant model of the DNA, which explained perfectly the observed rules of heredity, took the scientific world by storm. It brought to a conclusion an incomplete notion, suggested by Mendel eighty-eight years earlier, of a mechanism by which traits were passed on from generation to generation.

Watson, Crick and Wilkins were awarded the Nobel Prize in physiology/medicine in 1962. Rosalind Franklin, unfortunately, had died in 1958.

Charles Townes

An icon of our times is the laser. Truly a product of New Physics, for it was unthinkable before the first half of the twentieth century and the developments in atomic physics and quantum mechanics. The laser, which is a source of visible light with special properties, is based on the maser, an invention that created light waves like the laser, but of much lower frequency, in the microwave region. The first maser, or Microwaves Amplification by Stimulated Emission of Radiation, was built in 1953 by the American, Charles H. Townes, further to the work by Russians Nikolay Basov and Alexander Prokhorov.

Laser or maser light differs from ordinary light in the same way that a parade of marching soldiers differs from a crowd running down a street. The difference is that the soldiers are in step and their paces are in unison, unlike the crowd, whose feet strike the ground at different times. The timing of the marching soldiers sometimes matches the natural frequency of the oscillation of a bridge and the soldiers must break step, lest they bring the bridge down. Laser light, similarly, can become very intense. And laser light has the property of being highly directional, in the sense that a beam does not spread. And it is of a pure, single colour, owing to the way it comes about.

Townes was born in South Carolina in 1915. He completed his Masters in physics at Duke University and then joined Caltech, where he got his PhD in 1939. In 1950, he was appointed as professor in Columbia University, where he conceived of the maser the following year. In 1953, he, a graduate student and a colleague, built the ammonia maser.

The first artificial devices to create electromagnetic waves, of which light is an instance, were the antennas of radio transmitters. Electronic circuits generate rapidly alternating currents in the antenna, and the antenna sends out radio waves. As waves are created in sequence by the antenna, the waves are 'in step'. But radio waves spread in circles around the antenna; they are not directional.

Antennas are also many metres in length and so is the wavelength of radio waves. Electronic devices have been built to generate 'short waves', 'high frequency' waves and microwaves. But waves of sub-micron wavelength are not feasible with electronic devices. Waves of much shorter length are only created within atoms and molecules. While waves in the microwave and infrared regions arise in molecular transitions, visible light is emitted by electronic transitions of atoms.

The difference, however, is that atoms and molecules act individually, and emit waves in the infrared or visible regions, not in concert, but haphazardly. The atoms in the filament of a light bulb, for instance, emit light waves at random instants. It is the same in the case of emissions from the sun. Light from an electric bulb, a candle and sunlight are, thus, like the rushing crowd, while the waves from the radio antenna are like the marching troops.

The idea of the maser and the laser was to get molecules and atoms to emit light in unison, or in step, so that the infrared, or visible light, is coherent. Light like this would have use for communication, time keeping, digital recording and directionality. When the waves of light are in unison, the waves and the light can become very intense.

The concept, investigated by Basov and Prokhorov, and implemented by Townes, was an old suggestion by Einstein.

The concept was that if molecules in an excited state could be stimulated to emit a photon by another photon of the same frequency, then the two photons would set out together and be in unison. The practical device created by Townes made use of two energy levels in the molecules of ammonia gas (see Figure 34). The ammonia molecule consists of one nitrogen atom and three hydrogen atoms. The three hydrogen atoms are in a triangle and the nitrogen atom is in the middle, but to one side. When the gas is in an electric field, molecules where the nitrogen atom is on one side would have more energy than those where the nitrogen atom is on the other side. Flips from one side to the other side would continuously happen, with the emission or absorption of microwave photons. Now, if the molecules in the high-energy state could be separated, there would be more in higher energy than in the lower energy and a random photon could set off a cascade of photons. These would arise from stimulated emission, and hence they would be 'in step'!

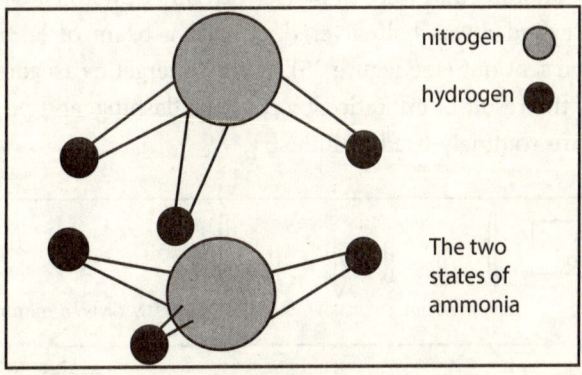

Figure 34

This is the concept of Townes's device of 1953, which led to the Nobel Prize for himself, Basov and Prokhorov, in 1964.

After the first maser in 1953, Townes and American physicist Arthur Leonard Schawlow adapted the maser to the visible part of the spectrum, by the stimulated emission of excited atoms by photons of visible light. In the ammonia maser, the condition of having more molecules in the higher-energy state was achieved by the separation of molecules. With electronic states of atoms, this was done by exciting atoms to a state that pauses a little before spontaneously de-exciting—a so-called meta-stable state. When atoms are excited to this state, there can be an accumulation of excited atoms. Any de-excitation, with emission, would stimulate a large number of atoms to de-excite, resulting in a cascade of emission.

The arrangement was to keep the material, which could be a gas or certain crystals, within or in the form of a cylinder with reflecting ends. When the material was energized by an electrical input, photons would reflect back and forth, and while atoms are pumped to the higher state, they would continue to be stimulated to emit photons that were in phase with other photons. One end of the cylinder was half-silvered, so that a beam of laser light could be sent out (see Figure 35). A very energetic cascade could also be the result of excitation by periodic flashing, and powerful lasers are routinely used in industry.

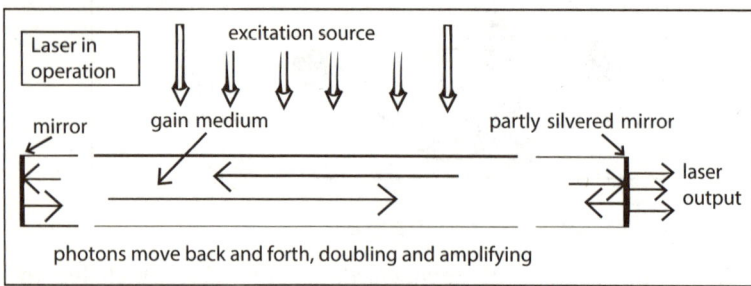

Figure 35

The source of the laser photons ensures that the laser is accurately at a single frequency, and the geometry of the arrangement ensures that the beam is highly directional. The laser is now the heart of optical cables and the means of writing and reading CDs and DVDs. Its heat is used for microsurgery, welding and metal cutting and laser beams are used in nuclear research and spectroscopy. Apart from its great utility, however, the laser is a validation of the models and the theory of a world that we can never hope to see.

Robert Holley, Marshall Nirenberg and Har Gobind Khorana

The saga of heredity, set in motion by Mendel in 1866, came to a glorious conclusion in 1953 with the discovery of DNA structure and the mechanism of genetic replication. The success, however, was incomplete, as the means for the transfer of genetic heritage in DNA into the physical characteristics of species and individuals was still unknown. This, too, was rapidly accomplished by the work of Robert Holley, Marshall Nirenberg and Har Gobind Khorana, recipients of the 1968 Nobel Prize for physiology or medicine.

Holley, born in 1922 in Urbana, Illinois, studied at the University of Illinois and Cornell and stayed on at Cornell. He said in his Nobel lecture, in 1968, that he had started work on RNA (a part of the cell related to the DNA) while at Caltech, on a sabbatical from Cornell, in 1955–56. Nirenberg was born in 1927 in New York, but he developed rheumatic fever and the family moved to Florida. He studied at the Universities of Florida and Michigan and then worked at the National Institute of Health at Bethesda, Maryland. Khorana was born in 1922 in Raipur, a small village in British India, now in Pakistan. He went to the Punjab University at Lahore and got a scholarship to pursue his PhD at the University of Liverpool. After working for a year at Zurich and some years at Cambridge, he moved to the University of Wisconsin at Madison.

The state of knowledge just after the structure of DNA

was found was that DNA consisted of a sugar and phosphate backbone with any one of just four distinct side chains, called G, C, A and T, attached continuously along the length of the molecule. It was also known that the character of organs, which collectively decide the character of a species, is regulated by the proteins that the cells of the organism produced. Further, it was found that all proteins consisted of a series, sometimes thousands-of-units long, of just twenty substances called amino acids.

Something in DNA, hence, was able to specify for an organism the order in which the amino acids were to be strung together for the vast number of proteins of organisms to be formed. Russian-born American physicist George Gamov suggested that groups of three of the side chains of DNA, where each side chain could take one of the four forms, could be the code to specify amino acids.

Now, a series of units, where each is one of four types, like words written with four letters, can exist in many forms. In a three-letter word, the first place can be any one of the four letters. For each choice of the first place, the second, again, can have four forms. This gives us 4 x 4 = 16 ways to fill the first two places. And then, with four ways to fill the third place, we have 16 x 4 = 64 ways in all. These sixty-four different codes can serve to identify twenty amino acids, along with alternate forms for the more common amino acids, to eliminate errors. But it remained to be proved that this is the way DNA coded amino acids and proteins.

Along with the genetic material later identified as DNA, which was discovered by Miescher in 1869, there was a version that was named RNA. In the 1900s, it was found that while DNA was inside the cell nucleus, RNA was in the fluid outside the nucleus. In the 1950s and '60s, it was found that bits of

DNA were transferred by RNA to structures that were outside the nucleus and these structures assembled proteins. In 1965, Holley, from Cornell University, uncovered the process by which the amino acid, aniline, by the action of RNA, got incorporated into proteins. Khorana, then at the Massachusetts Institute of Technology, worked on ways to build RNA according to need, and to isolate RNA, which helped build specific proteins.

In 1965, Nirenberg and his students used the material of a ruptured bacterial cell, where the DNA had been denatured, as a medium for building proteins. As the DNA had been destroyed, any synthesis of proteins, by linking amino acids together, would depend on the nature of the RNA that was added. Several trials, requiring challenging conditions to control purity and temperature, were carried out with synthetic RNA and twenty separate sources of pure amino acids. One of the twenty amino acids had a radioactive marker, in succession, in each trial. This was to see if a particular amino acid was picked up to form the protein that resulted.

The experiment showed that with the RNA, Poly U, which contained only the side chain, U (this is the RNA form of the DNA side chain, T), the RNA picked out the amino acid, phenyl aniline, to form the protein, polyphenylaniline, a chain of just this amino acid. This was a first step in cracking the code: that 'UUU' was the code for the amino acid, phenyl aniline. This was a breakthrough—a demonstration that DNA contained the code for the formation of a protein and a way to extract the code and assemble a protein.

Khorana, who had been working on the synthesis of RNA, took on the task of creating more RNA. Nirenberg had shown that the chain, UUUUU..., created polyphenylaniline. In the same way, the sequence, CCCCC..., created a protein consisting of the amino acid, proline. The sequence, AAAAA..., created polylysine. Khorana used a more complex RNA, UGUGUGUG..., to create a mixture of valine, UGU (or TGT), and cystine, GUG (or GTG). And the sequence, UCUCUCUC..., led to serine (UCU) and leucine (CUC). In this way, with the increasing complexity of experiments, all sixty-one triplets that code for amino acids were worked out (three triples, UAA, UAG and UGA, do not code amino acids but indicate the 'end' of a list of amino acids).

The work of Holley, Nirenberg and Khorana created a sensation when it was announced. Genetics became a major area of research. The code had been found but now it had to be made use of. Methods were developed for the manipulation of bits of DNA. In the 1980s, a programme was started to map the human genome, which has 3 billion base pairs over its length. The mapping was completed in the early 2000s.

Since then, knowledge has increased by leaps and bounds. Methods have been found to snip and splice specific locations in the DNA. Genetic bases of many diseases have been determined, and those affected can be treated or helped to adapt. In agriculture, genetic intervention has multiplied the produce of foodgrain, and helped plants resist pests or drought. There are prospects of getting microbes to clear pollution, process chemicals, and even use sunlight to generate power. Gene technology is being used in industry and genetics may be the most important science in the twenty-first century.

Afterword

After the flurry of developments in science from the fifteenth century to the middle of the twentieth century, the last half century gives the impression of science being back to groping for direction.

There have been important discoveries about the cosmos—that the universe is expanding, after its beginning in the 'big bang', a short period of rapid expansion from a point source. But there are questions of what sustains the expansion, the mystery of why galaxies spin faster at the extremities and why there are two sciences—quantum mechanics for the very small and General Relativity for the very large.

The field of genetics has taken large strides and many view biotechnology as the answer to the world's need for food, power and restoring the environment, in the century to follow. Nanotechnology and information science may also usher in powerful ways of managing resources.

New directions in science in the coming decades may have answers that we cannot even imagine. It may have been the same during earlier stages of the development of science, when what would be discovered next could not be foreseen.